JAPANESE GARNISHES

YUKIKO AND BOB HAYDOCK

JAPANESE GARNISHES

THE ANCIENT ART OF MUKIMONO

HOLT, RINEHART AND WINSTON · NEW YORK

Published by Holt, Rinehart and Winston,
383 Madison Avenue, New York, New York 10017.
Published simultaneously in Canada by
Holt, Rinehart and Winston of Canada, Limited.

Library of Congress Cataloging in Publication Data
Haydock, Yukiko.
Japanese garnishes.
1. Cookery (Garnishes)   2. Cookery, Japanese.
1. Haydock, Bob, joint author.   II.   Title.
TX652.H394   641.5   80-13851
ISBN 0-03-048236-4

Illustrations and photographs by Bob Haydock
Design by Amy Hill and Bob Haydock

Printed in the United States of America
10 9 8 7 6 5 4

CONTENTS

FOREWORD

I first met the authors in late 1978 when they were on a research trip to Japan. They came to visit me at my restaurant in Tokyo to discuss Mukimono. I was delighted with their enthusiasm for this traditional Japanese art as well as with their intention to adapt some of the simpler designs to Western cuisine.

In Japan, the chef's technique in the use of knives is called Kaishiki. Mukimono, or the art of vegetable peeling, is a most important part of this traditional technique. It is an expression of the pleasure and delight in handmade things. In these hectic days, I hope this little book will help to reawaken a love for these simple pleasures.

I find it meaningful for a book like this to be published in a foreign country, and it gives me much happiness to know that it will help you add beauty and fantasy to your table.

HITOSHI MORIMOTO

Chairman of the Board of Directors, Daikyo Kansai Chef's Association; Master, Society for Research of Japanese Cuisine; Master, Japanese Professional Chef's Society; Master, Kansai Chef's League; and Instructor, Japanese Ministry of Labor Chef's Training Program.

PLE FEATHER

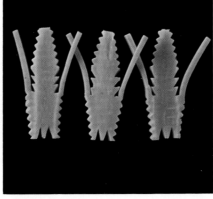

CARROT TWISTS

CARROT CURLS

RROT BLOSSOMS

CARROT CORN

CUCUMBER CHAIN

CUMBER TWIGS

CUCUMBER LOOPS

CUCUMBER SPRING

SHOOTING STAR

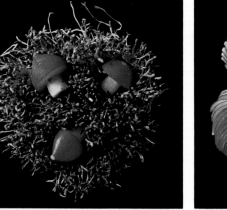

FLYING FISH

SPANISH COMB

EGG FROG

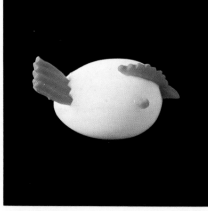

EGG CHICKEN

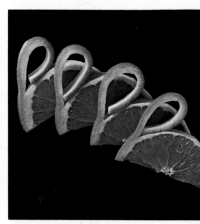

ORANGE LOOPS

RADISH BUDS

RADISH MUSHROOMS

RADISH FAN

DISH JACKS

RADISH BLOSSOM

TOMATO BUTTERFLY

MATO CAMELIA

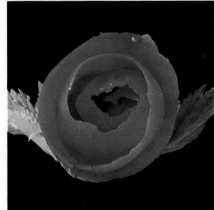

TOMATO ROSE

TOMATO ARTICHOKE

RNIP CHICKS

TURNIP NETTLES

TURNIP MUM

SQUASH FEATHER

ZUCCHINI PALM

ZUCCHINI DAISY

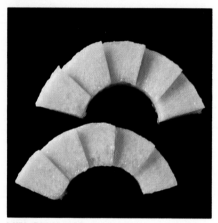

MELON FANS

MAPLE LEAF

ONION FLOWER

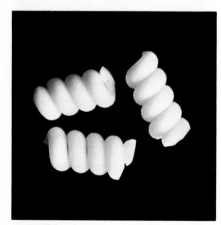

POTATO SPRING

SCALLION BRUSH

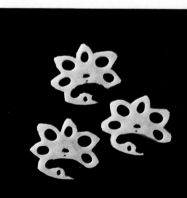

LOTUS PEACOCK

INTRODUCTION

Serving food attractively is an art that has been practiced for centuries. Most of the garnishes we have selected originate in Japan. The Japanese have brought the same exquisite sense of taste and refinement to garnishing that they have brought to other art forms. *Mukimono* means ''the art of vegetable peeling,'' and we have chosen to use it in our title, although we hasten to say that this book is hardly an authoritative treatise on that ancient Japanese art. We have simplified the techniques enormously to make the garnishes fairly easy to prepare in Western kitchens. All of the garnishes in this book can be made by novices as well as by more experienced cooks.

Mukimono's origins date back to ancient times when food first began to be served on unglazed clay pottery. The pottery was first covered with a leaf upon which the food was placed. It wasn't long before a chef/artist realized that by cutting or folding the leaf in different ways, a more attractive presentation could be made. And so Mukimono began. But it wasn't until the 1720s, during the Tokugawa Era, that it became quite popular. During this period, when Edo (Tokyo) became the new capital, Mukimono gained official recognition. In fact, Mukimono so charmed everyone that street artists would amuse their customers (for a small fee) by creating clever garnishes upon request. From those beginnings, the art has developed into a most important part of every Japanese chef's training.

We have tried to use a wide assortment of fruits and vegetables to show various Mukimono techniques. Since the book is arranged by food category, you can turn to whatever food you feel like using and find numerous garnish ideas. The majority of the garnishes don't require any equipment more special than a sharp paring knife, but any other tools needed are listed in the section that follows.

We hope you will use the ideas in this book to show your guests that you are glad they have come by adding a personal touch to the meal you serve them.

TOOLS

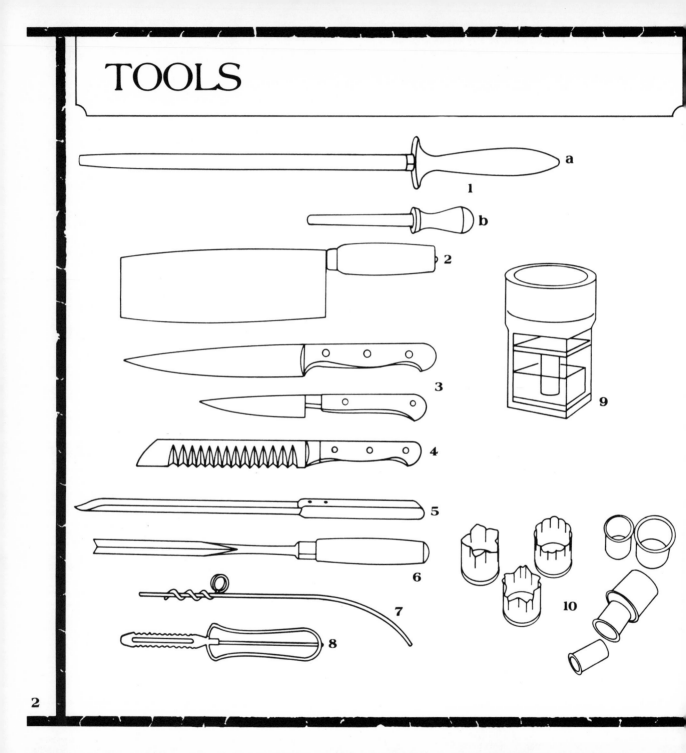

In all skills tools are important, and Mukimono is no exception. The illustration shows all the tools you will need. For the most part, the garnishes don't require unusual tools. Ordinary kitchen paring knives will usually suffice. In a few cases we have included garnishes that do call for special tools, and these can be found in most kitchen supply stores.

1. **KNIFE SHARPENERS.** The first rule in using knives is to always keep them sharp. The classic way to accomplish this is with the sharpening steel (la), a round, tapered, hard-chromed steel bar with a handle and hilt usually about 20 inches long overall. A newcomer is the small Zip-Zap ceramic sharpener (lb). It is held between the thumb and forefinger and moved across the blade diagonally. It is an excellent sharpener, and since it is only about 5½ inches long it can be kept handy.

2. **JAPANESE CHEF'S KNIFE.** This shouldn't be confused with a cleaver, which it might resemble in the drawing. It is actually quite lightweight. The blade, although broad, is as thin as a conventional paring knife. The broad blade is helpful in making garnishes that require a long peeling cut, such as the Radish Net (see page 64). The knife is generally available only in Oriental cutlery stores. If you do not live near one, try using a paring knife with the widest blade you can find.

3. **PARING KNIVES.** Most garnishes can be made with these conventional kitchen knives. They are relatively inexpensive, so it pays to buy good ones. Avoid the dime-store variety in favor of forged, high-carbon, nonstaining steel. A good knife will sharpen easily and stay sharp. The blade will not chip but will be flexible and have a well-pointed tip. Also, the handle will not loosen and pull away from the blade. Two knives are all you'll need: one with a 4–5-inch blade and one with a 2–3-inch blade.

4. **GARNISH KNIFE.** This specialty knife is available in most kitchen supply stores. The blade is not flat but zigzags from left to right. A potato cut in half with this knife will have a ribbed surface.

5. **ZUCCHINI CORER.** This is another specialty instrument, but it shouldn't be hard to find. Its blade is a one-third cylinder with a pointed tip. It is just the right tool for coring long vegetables, such as zucchini.

6. **V-SHAPED CHISEL.** This is not a cooking shop item. For this you will have to visit the local hardware store. The one we use is 8½ inches in overall length, with a ¼-inch V.

7. **POTATO CUTTER.** This gadget is so unusual that it makes you wonder how anyone could have thought it up. But someone did, and it works beautifully (see Potato Spring, page 98). It should be available in most kitchen supply stores.

8. **VEGETABLE PEELER.** This is one of the most familiar kitchen gadgets. It is also one of the cheapest and has yet to be improved upon. It cannot be resharpened, however, so a new one should be purchased when it becomes dull.

9. **SQUARE EGG MOLD.** This is simply a clear plastic molding device. A warm boiled egg is inserted into the mold, the top is screwed down, and the egg is left to cool. When cool, the egg will retain its square shape. The square egg-maker is made in Japan and imported by Cost Plus Imports, 2552 Taylor Street, San Francisco, California.

10. **GARNISH CUTTERS.** These are known as truffle cutters, aspic cutters, biscuit cutters, and cookie cutters. For our purposes, we will refer to them all as garnish cutters. Essentially, the cutting edge is formed into a design, such as a circle, star, or animal. There are even cutters that shape every letter of the alphabet. Garnish cutters are available in kitchen supply stores. Some sets can be quite expensive—over $100. Fortunately, there are also much cheaper ones.

APPLE BUNNY

One of the things that Mukimono teaches is how little it takes to transform one thing into something quite different. A couple of quick cuts, and an apple wedge becomes a bunny rabbit!

SERVING SUGGESTIONS: Of course, the Apple Bunny is a natural for Easter. It's also at home on any fruit salad, as a garnish for a cheese tray, or served with sandwiches.

YOU WILL NEED: large red apple, paring knife, bowl of Fruit-Fresh solution.

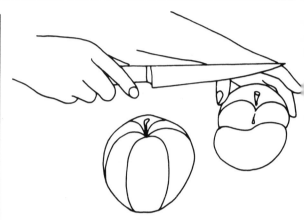

1. Cut a nice red apple into six wedges.

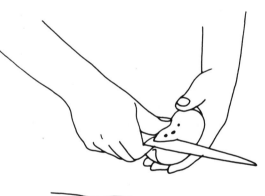

2. Remove the core from each wedge.

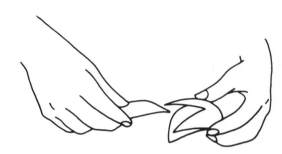

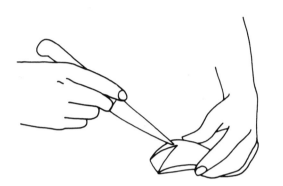

3. Make two cuts as shown. The cuts should just penetrate the skin.

5. Remove the piece between the two cuts to form the ears.

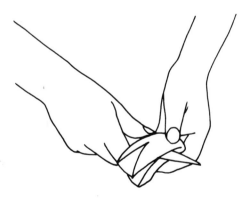

4. Slice the skin away from the apple to about 1 inch from the end.

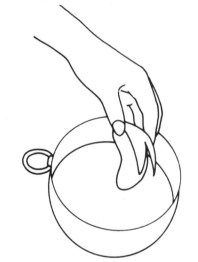

6. Soak in a solution of Fruit-Fresh (mix 2 tablespoons per cup of water) for 2 minutes. (Fruit-Fresh is a commercial product available in grocery stores. It will keep the apple from turning brown. Rubbing lemon juice on the apple will also work, but we recommend using Fruit-Fresh because it imparts no taste.)

APPLE FEATHER

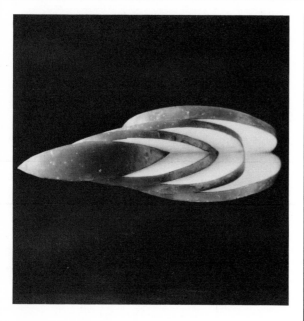

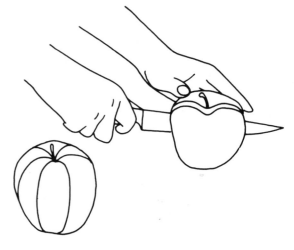

1. Cut an apple into six wedges.

The Apple Feather is made by cutting an apple wedge into four V-shaped slices. The slices are then put back together but spread out a little for an interesting effect.

SERVING SUGGESTIONS: Apple Feathers can accompany a cheese tray or be used in a fruit salad.

YOU WILL NEED: large red apple, paring knife, bowl of Fruit-Fresh solution.

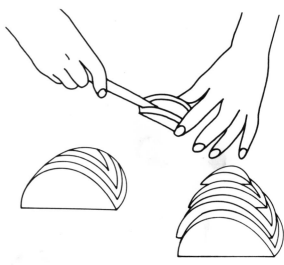

2. Cut each wedge into four layered V-shaped slices, as shown.

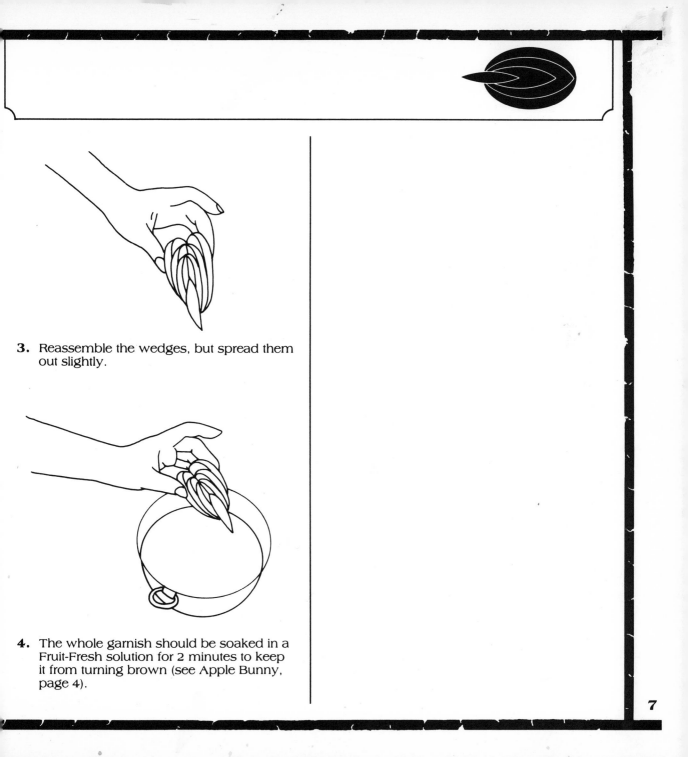

3. Reassemble the wedges, but spread them out slightly.

4. The whole garnish should be soaked in a Fruit-Fresh solution for 2 minutes to keep it from turning brown (see Apple Bunny, page 4).

STARWHEELS

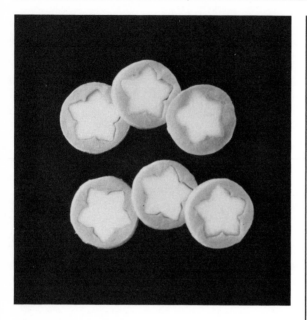

Starwheels will require a garnish cutter. We are using a star-shaped one, but other shapes can be just as interesting. Carrots should be at room temperature, since cold carrots are brittle and harder to cut.

SERVING SUGGESTIONS: Starwheels can be put into a mixed green salad or used as a garnish for potato salad.

YOU WILL NEED: carrot and large white radish or turnip, paring knife, vegetable peeler, star-shaped garnish cutter.

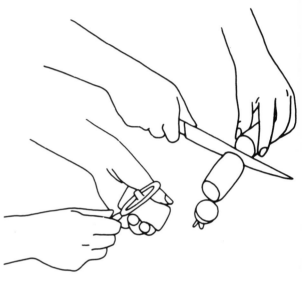

1. Cut a 3-inch section from a large carrot. (The diameter of the carrot should be wider than that of the cutter being used.) Peel it with a vegetable peeler.

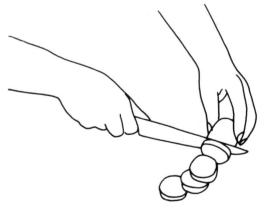

2. Slice the carrot into ⅜-inch-thick slices.

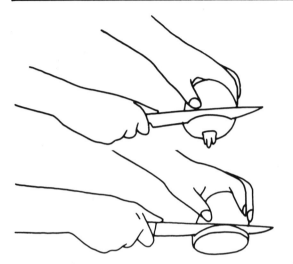

3. Cut a ⅜-inch slice from a large white radish or turnip.

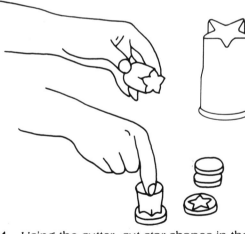

4. Using the cutter, cut star shapes in the carrot slices.

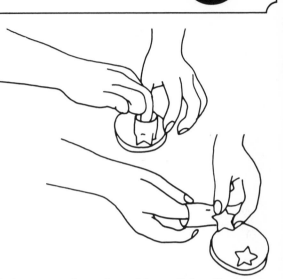

5. Cut stars from the white radish with the cutter.

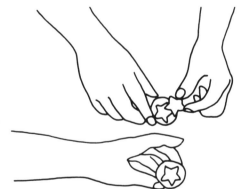

6. Insert the white radish star into the carrot and there it is—a Starwheel. (Note: You can make large Starwheels by using the leftovers. Fit the leftover carrot star shapes into the star holes in the white radish slice.)

CARROT SPURS

Carrot Spurs are similar to Starwheels, but you won't need any special tools for these.

SERVING SUGGESTIONS: Carrot Spurs can be mixed into a green salad or served with a dip. They can also be cooked and served as a vegetable dish. Or, you can cook them slightly and add them to a potato salad.

YOU WILL NEED: carrot, paring knife, V-shaped chisel, vegetable peeler.

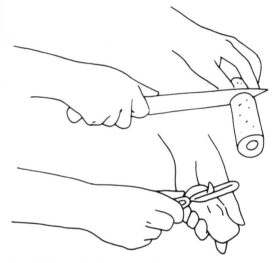

1. Cut a 3-inch section from a carrot, and peel it with a vegetable peeler.

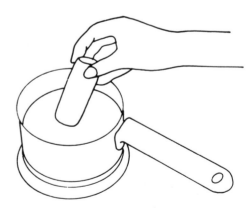

2. Cook the carrot in boiling water for about 4 minutes. This will soften it and make your carving job much easier.

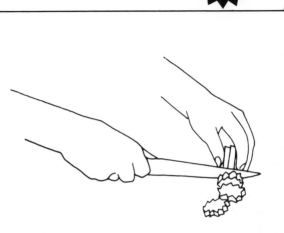

4. From this basic carved shape, cut individual Carrot Spur slices.

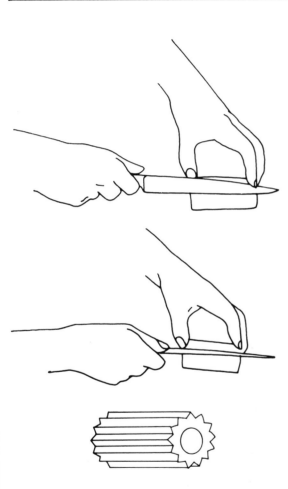

3. Once the carrot has cooled, cut lengthwise triangular grooves around it with a knife or V-shaped chisel. These cuts should be about ⅛ inch deep.

11

CARROT TWISTS

The Carrot Twist is another of those simple little transformations that are so delightful in Mukimono. As always, whenever a vegetable is to be curled to any degree, it should be soaked in a salt solution for at least 10 minutes.

SERVING SUGGESTIONS: Carrot Twists can be scattered through a green salad or used to garnish a sandwich plate. They can also be cooked slightly and dropped in hot consommé.

YOU WILL NEED: carrot, paring knife, vegetable peeler, bowl of salt solution.

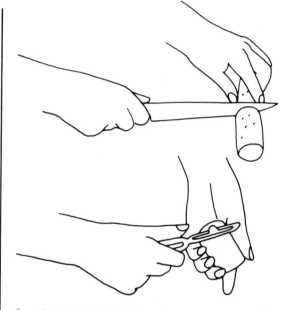

1. Cut a 3-inch section from a carrot, and peel it with a vegetable peeler.

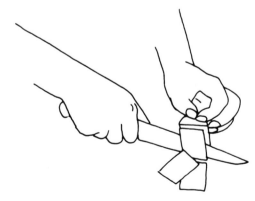

2. Cut the section into ⅛-inch-thick slices.

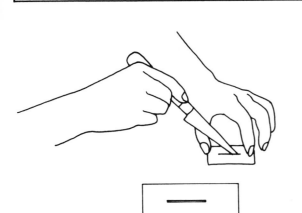

3. Make a 1-inch slit in the center of each slice.

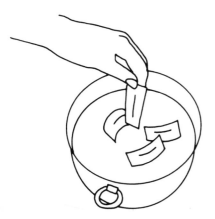

4. Soak the pieces in a salt solution (1 tablespoon salt, 1 quart water) for at least 10 minutes. Rinse.

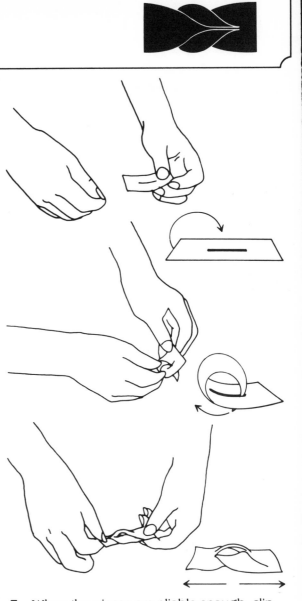

5. When the pieces are pliable enough, slip one end of each piece through the slit in the center and pull it straight back.

CARROT CURLS

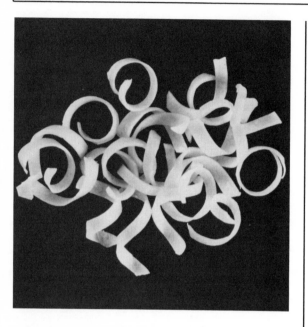

Carrot Curls look easy to make, but they are a bit deceiving. The problem comes in peeling the long, flat strip from the carrot. The best tool for this task is the Japanese chef's knife. The carrot should be turned into the blade while the knife is held steady.

SERVING SUGGESTIONS: Carrot Curls can be sprinkled on a green salad or used as a nest to surround a serving of egg salad.

YOU WILL NEED: carrot, paring knife, vegetable peeler, Japanese chef's knife, bowl of ice water.

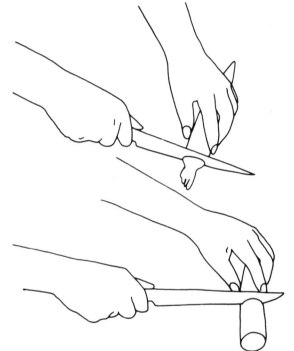

1. Cut a 3-inch section from a carrot, and peel it with a vegetable peeler.

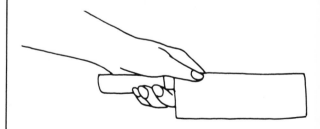

2. A Japanese chef's knife should be used for the next cut (see Tools, page 2).

14

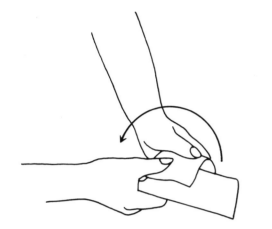

3. Using the chef's knife, peel a thin sheet from the carrot. For easier curling, the thinner the slice the better.

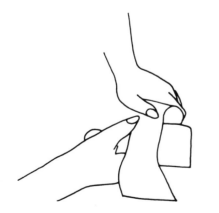

4. The carrot should be turned into the blade. The blade can then be rocked back and forth gently and a slight pressure applied with the left thumb. Cut as long and as thin a sheet as possible.

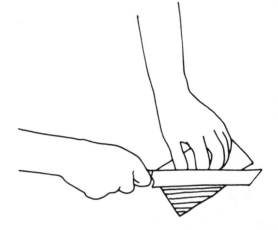

5. Cut the sheet into diagonal ¼-inch-wide strips. The diagonal cut will allow the carrot strips to curl easier.

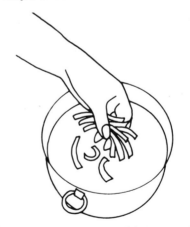

6. Place the strips in ice cold water. This is what causes the curling. (Note: Carrot Curls cannot be cooked or they will flatten out.)

CARROT BLOSSOMS

The Carrot Blossom is one in our bouquet of flower garnishes. It's small, edible, and can be used either cooked or raw.

SERVING SUGGESTIONS: Cook in boiling water for about 2 minutes, and float on a serving of chicken-and-rice soup, consomme, or split pea soup. Or place several on a filet of sole with mornay sauce.

YOU WILL NEED: carrot, paring knife, metal skewer, V-shaped chisel.

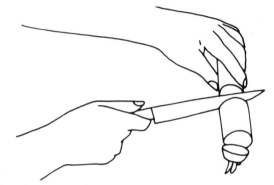

1. Cut a 3-inch section from a carrot.

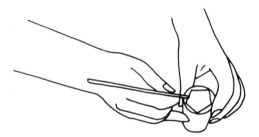

2. Draw a pentagon on one end, using either the point of the knife or a skewer. This will be used as a guide for cutting.

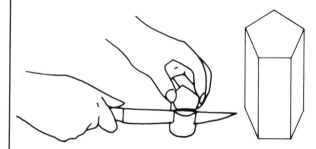

3. Slice the five sides from the carrot, following the outline guide.

16

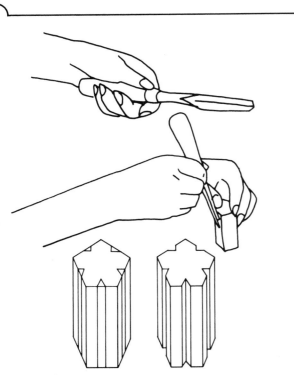

4. With a knife or V-shaped chisel, make five lengthwise cuts as shown. These cuts will shape the flower.

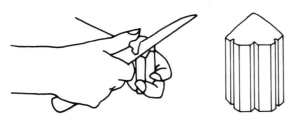

5. Shape one end of the carrot so that the center is slightly higher than the edges.

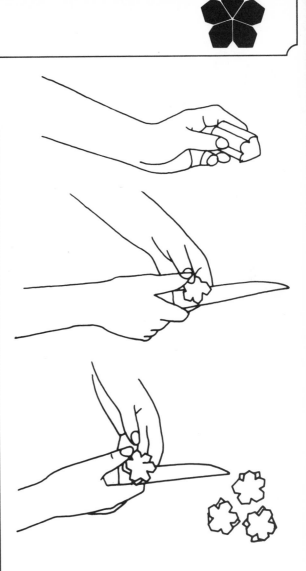

6. The flower petals can now be sliced from this end, as shown. Use a thin peeling cut, turning the carrot into the knife blade. Go around twice to create a double petal.

CARROT CORN

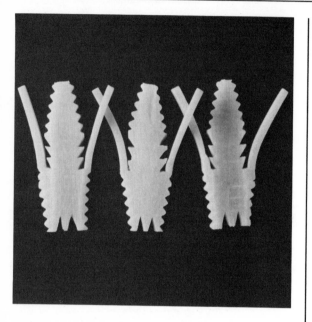

Carrot Corn and Carrot Spurs are made in much the same way. The principle is to carve a basic shape and then slice it into many individual garnishes.

SERVING SUGGESTIONS: Cook in boiling water or chicken broth for 5 minutes. Drain. Season with salt, pepper, and melted butter. Use to surround a roast chicken, roast pork, or a roast beef on a serving platter, or place on top of an omelet or on rolled cabbages.

YOU WILL NEED: carrot, paring knife, garnish knife.

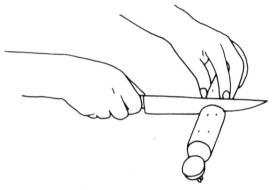

1. Cut a 3-inch section from a large carrot. (The carrot should be at room temperature. Cold carrots become brittle and are harder to cut.)

2. Slice off the sides in four cuts so that a rectangular center remains.

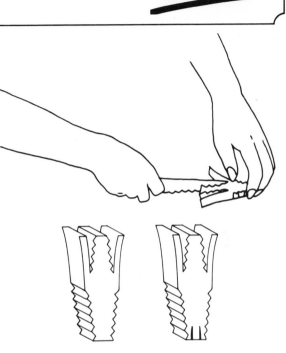

3. First make two cuts through the carrot as shown. Push the two sides away from the center piece.

4. Use a garnish knife to make the serrated edges (see Tools, page 2). Cut both sides of the base, as shown.

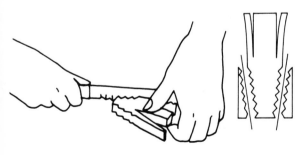

5. Next, cut both sides of the center piece and notch the bottom.

6. Individual garnishes may now be sliced from the carved block.

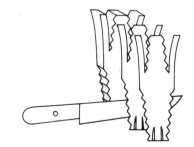

CUCUMBER CHAIN

This is one of the easiest garnishes to make, and since the chain can be any length, it can be used in lots of different ways. It's a tasty garnish, especially when marinated in sweet and sour dressing.

SERVING SUGGESTIONS: Use to encircle a tuna salad, or drop in a cold cucumber soup or on top of a cucumber salad. Cucumber chains also go well with chicken salad or shrimp or crab Louis.

YOU WILL NEED: cucumber, zucchini corer, paring knife, round garnish cutter.

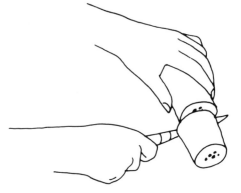

1. Cut a 3–4-inch cylinder from a large cucumber.

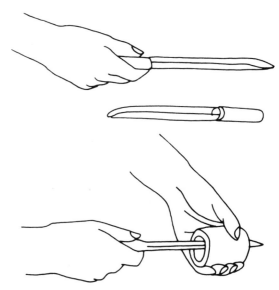

2. Remove the core with either a regular paring knife or a zucchini corer (see Tools, page 2).

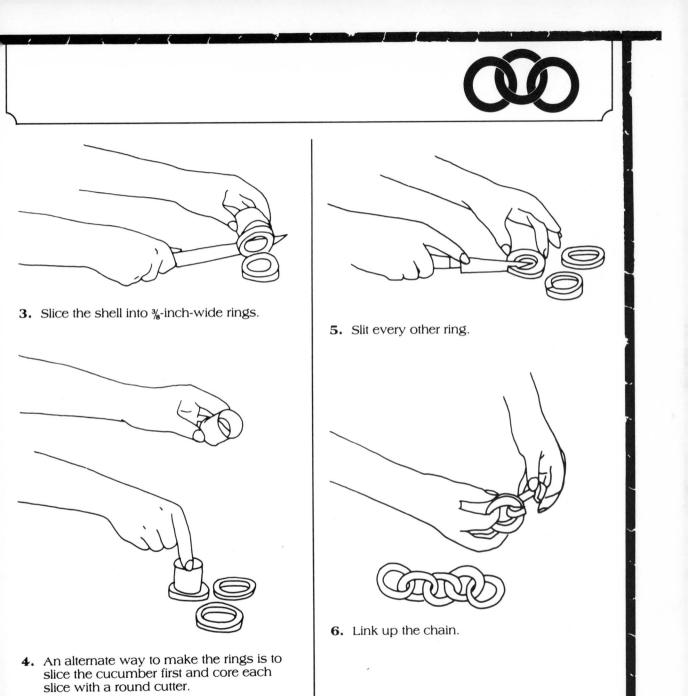

3. Slice the shell into ⅜-inch-wide rings.

5. Slit every other ring.

4. An alternate way to make the rings is to slice the cucumber first and core each slice with a round cutter.

6. Link up the chain.

CUCUMBER TWIGS

The Cucumber Twig is another one of our favorite garnishes. Its appeal lies in its simplicity. The best Mukimono is always the simplest. You may also use carrots for the contrast in color.

SERVING SUGGESTIONS: Sprinkle several over cold cucumber soup, or use as a garnish on aspics, cold meats, and luncheon salads. Cucumber Twigs may also be served with a dip.

YOU WILL NEED: cucumber, paring knife.

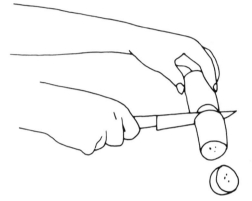

1. Cut a 2-inch section from an unpeeled cucumber.

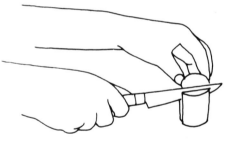

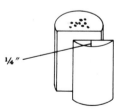

¼"

2. Slice off one side, as shown. This piece should be about ¼ inch thick.

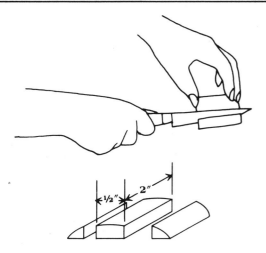

3. Cut a center section—about ½ inch wide by 2 inches long—from this slice.

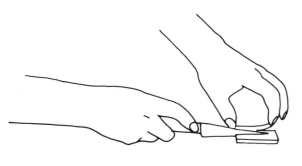

4. Make two lengthwise cuts; one from each end as shown. (Note: Neither cut goes all the way through the piece; about ¼ inch should be left at each end.)

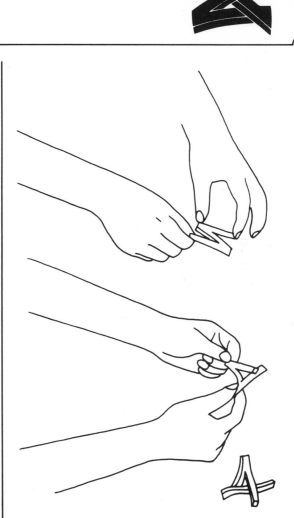

5. Twist the two outer legs so they cross each other.

CUCUMBER CUPS

These little cups can be made quite easily from a cucumber. They are also easy to make in large quantities. Again, as with the Cucumber Twigs, simplicity is the key.

SERVING SUGGESTIONS: By all means, these cups are functional as well as decorative. Try filling them with mayonnaise, tartar sauce, horseradish, or cranberry sauce. You might even try salmon caviar for a nice color contrast.

YOU WILL NEED: cucumber, paring knife, spoon.

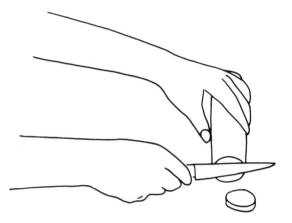

1. Cut the end from an unpeeled cucumber. The larger the cucumber, the bigger the cup.

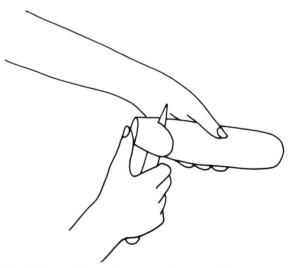

2. Make a slanted cut, as shown, about 2 inches from the end.

3. Make two more of these cuts around the circumference of the cucumber, a total of three cuts.

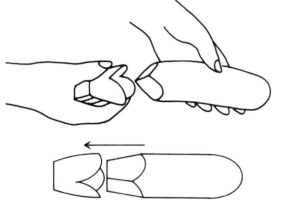

4. That's all there is. The cup can be easily removed from the cucumber.

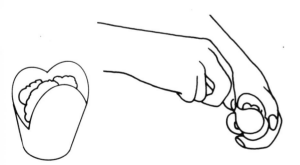

5. The inside of the cup can be scooped out with a spoon if you wish it to hold more.

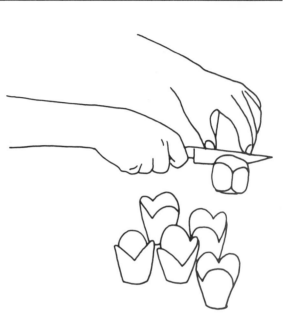

6. Additional cups can be made from the same cucumber by repeating the three cuts. Remember to cut the end of the cucumber flat before starting again.

CUCUMBER DIPPERS

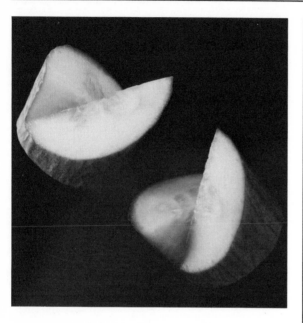

Although this looks like a complicated cut, it really isn't. Once you get the knack, you'll be able to turn out Cucumber Dippers by the dozens.

SERVING SUGGESTIONS: These elegant Cucumber Dippers are best used as hors d'oeuvres, eaten fresh with a dip. This is also a decorative way to cut zucchini or carrots before cooking them.

YOU WILL NEED: cucumber, two paring knives.

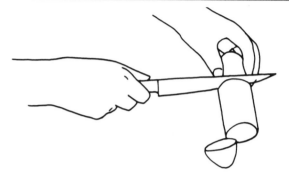

1. Cut a 3-inch section from a narrow cucumber. Do not peel it.

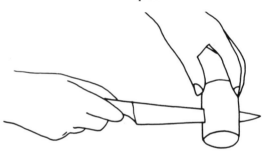

2. Insert a knife through the center. The blade should be about 1 inch wide.

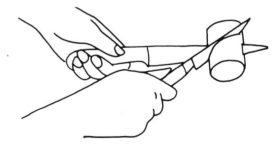

3. Make a diagonal cut with another knife all the way to the first knife.

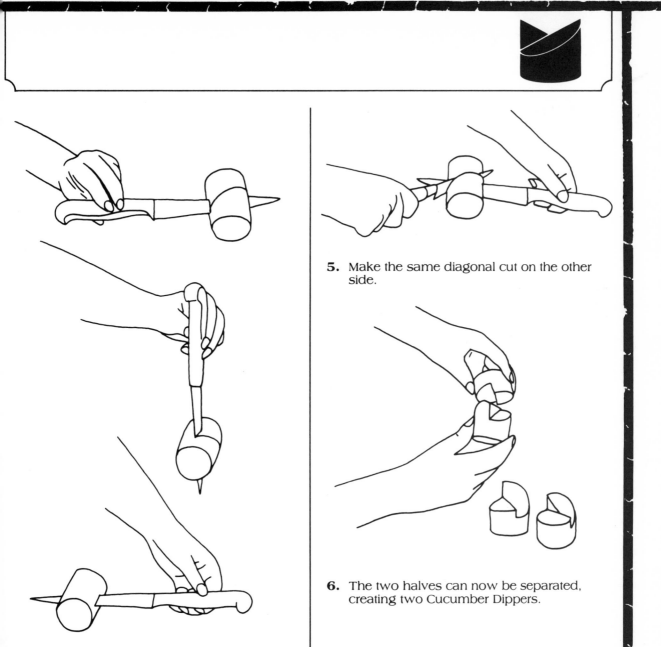

5. Make the same diagonal cut on the other side.

6. The two halves can now be separated, creating two Cucumber Dippers.

4. Now turn the cucumber over, as shown.

CUCUMBER LOOPS

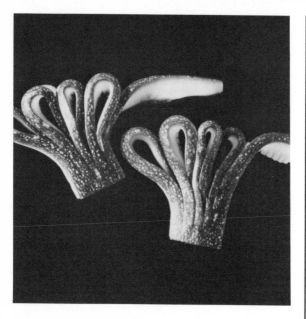

The Cucumber Loop is another garnish that requires a thorough soaking in a salt solution to make it more pliable.

SERVING SUGGESTIONS: Place two or three of these on a serving of tomato or seafood salad. Garnish a platter of batter-fried fish, or place on top of egg salad sandwiches.

YOU WILL NEED: cucumber, paring knife, bowl of salt solution.

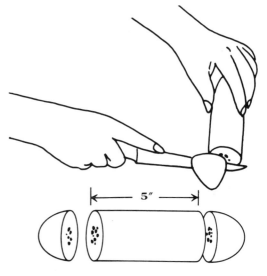

1. Cut a 5-inch section from a large, unpeeled cucumber.

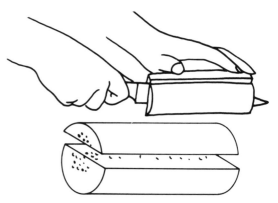

2. Make a lengthwise cut, slicing off about one-third of the section. This smaller piece will be used for the garnishes.

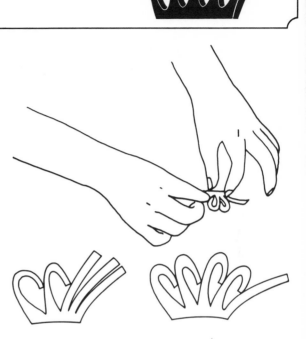

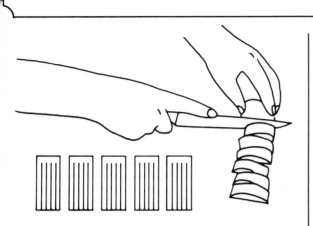

3. Place this piece of cucumber flat side down, and cut it into sections, as shown. Each section should be about 1 inch thick. Make four equally spaced cuts in each section, being sure to leave a narrow spine to hold the section together.

5. Fold the first four strips over to make the loops. Leave the last one straight.

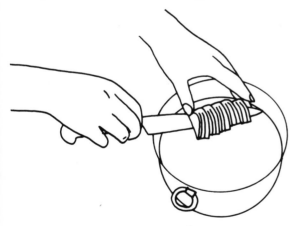

4. Soak the sections in a salt solution (1 tablespoon salt, 1 quart water) for at least 10 minutes, or until they can be easily manipulated. Rinse.

CUCUMBER BOWS

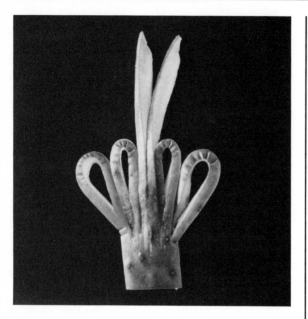

More cucumber magic. The Cucumber Bow will need a 10-minute soaking in a salt solution for best results.

SERVING SUGGESTIONS: Garnish a salmon steak. Use with eggs in aspic or stuffed eggs. Use on hot or cold meats, chicken, or fish. Sprinkle over a tomato salad.

YOU WILL NEED: cucumber, paring knife, bowl of salt solution.

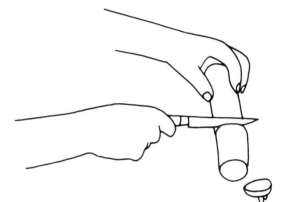

1. Cut a 4-inch section from an unpeeled cucumber.

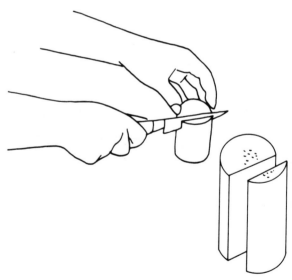

2. Slice off 1 side, as shown, about ⅜ inch thick.

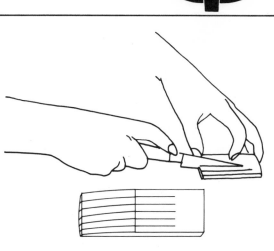

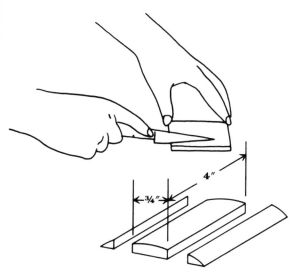

3. Cut out the center section to form a piece about ⅜ inch thick by ¾ inch wide by 4 inches long.

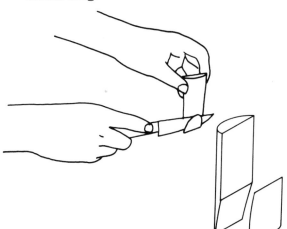

4. Shave one end as shown.

5. Make five lengthwise cuts, starting at the shaved end, as shown. These cuts should extend to about 1 inch from the other end.

6. Soak the cucumber in a salt solution (1 tablespoon salt, 1 quart water) for at least 10 minutes. Rinse.

7. Fold the leaves into a bow design, as shown.

CUCUMBER SPRING

There is a gadget available in most kitchen supply shops that will make this garnish in a flash. But we thought we would show you how to do it the old-fashioned way.

SERVING SUGGESTIONS: Cucumber Springs can be used in a green salad or in a cucumber vinaigrette. Short ones can be used on trays of cold cuts to encircle rolled slices of ham or sticks of cheese.

YOU WILL NEED: cucumber, paring knife, chopstick.

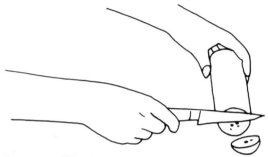

1. Cut off both ends of an unpeeled cucumber.

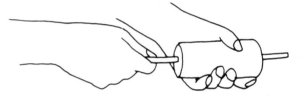

2. Insert a chopstick through the center.

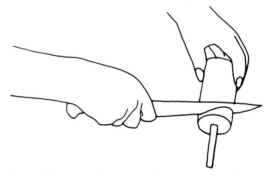

3. Make your first cut all the way to the center of the cucumber (to the chopstick) and at a slight angle. Leave the knife in this position.

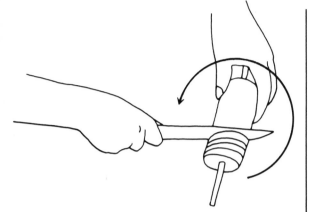

4. Slowly begin turning the cucumber toward you so that the knife cuts the entire length of the cucumber.

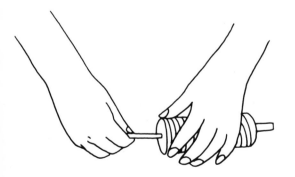

5. Remove the chopstick.

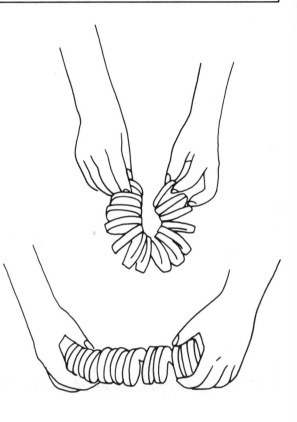

6. This garnish is as flexible as a spring and can be arranged on the plate in lots of different ways.

SHOOTING STAR

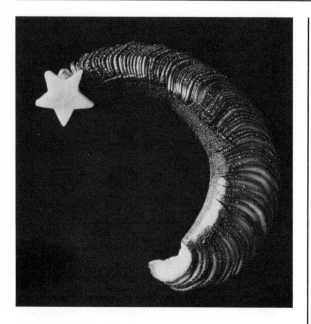

The Shooting Star will test your patience. Its success depends upon your making a multitude of little slices along the length of a cucumber. They will transform the cucumber into a graceful, curving shape.

SERVING SUGGESTIONS: The Shooting Star is primarily a decorative garnish and not really meant to be eaten. It is a dramatic addition to any serving platter.

YOU WILL NEED: cucumber, paring knife, bowl of salt solution, star-shaped garnish cutter.

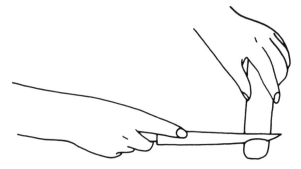

1. Cut the ends off an unpeeled cucumber.

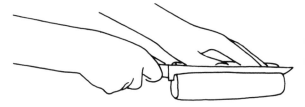

2. Slice the body in half, lengthwise.

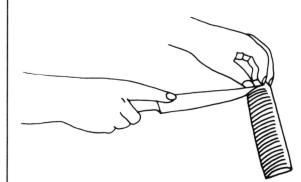

3. Make a series of slices about ⅛ inch thick down the length of one half, leaving a ¼-inch spine to hold the slices together.

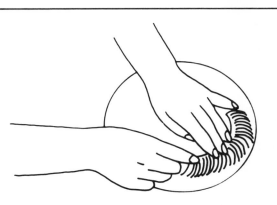

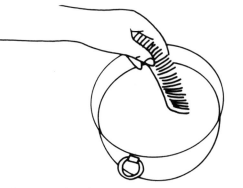

4. Soak in a salt solution (1 tablespoon salt, 1 quart water) at least 10 minutes. Rinse.

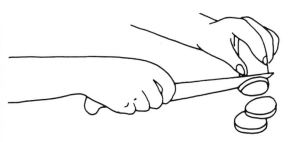

5. Cut a carrot slice about ⅛ inch thick.

6. Punch out a star, using a star-shaped cutter (see Tools, page 2).

7. Spread the cucumber out on the serving plate.

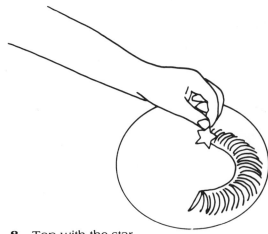

8. Top with the star.

FLYING FISH

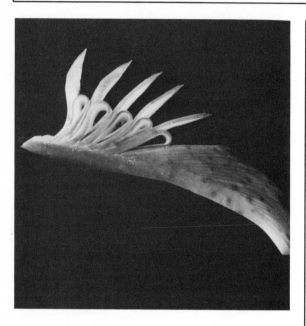

The key to this garnish, as to several others, is to soak it in a salt solution. This will make it pliable enough to manipulate with ease.

SERVING SUGGESTIONS: One Flying Fish at each end of a serving platter will frame the entree nicely. Lay a Flying Fish along the top of a poached salmon, or curve one across the top of a round serving platter of cold cuts.

YOU WILL NEED: cucumber, paring knife, bowl of salt solution.

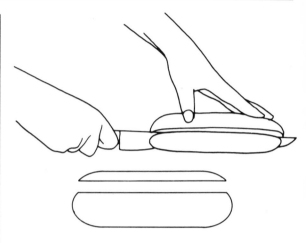

1. Slice the cucumber in about a ⅓ to ⅔ ratio. Use a large seedless cucumber if available.

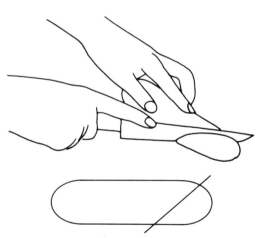

2. Place the thinner piece flat side down on the cutting board, and slice off one end at about a 30-degree angle.

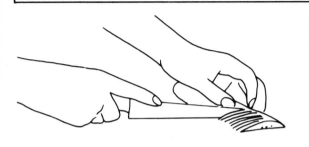

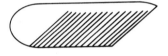

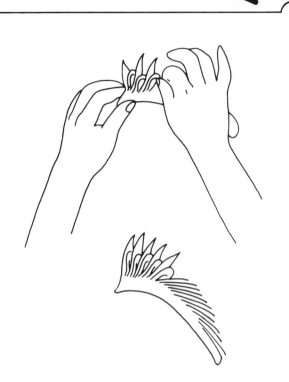

3. Keeping the piece flat side down, make a series of diagonal slices about ⅛ inch apart down its length. Be sure to leave a spine so the slices stay together.

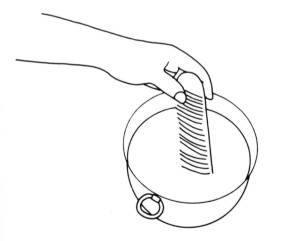

5. Fold under five or six alternating slices to create the Flying Fish effect.

4. Soak the cucumber in a salt solution (1 tablespoon salt, 1 quart water) for at least 10 minutes. Rinse.

SPANISH COMB

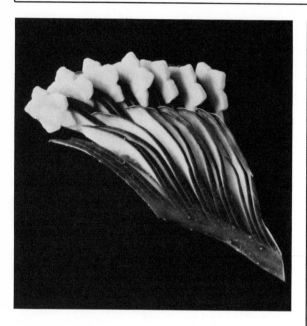

The Spanish Comb is created by slicing a cucumber in the same diagonal manner as the Flying Fish (see page 36). The addition of the carrot stars makes it a little more festive and colorful. Again, the cucumber will be easier to work with if it is first soaked in a salt solution.

SERVING SUGGESTIONS: In spite of its name, this is a garnish that seems right for a 4th of July or New Year's Eve party.

YOU WILL NEED: cucumber, carrot, paring knife, star-shaped garnish cutter.

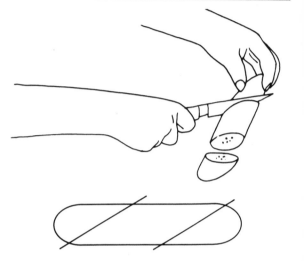

1. Remove the ends of an unpeeled cucumber, making diagonal cuts of about 30 degrees.

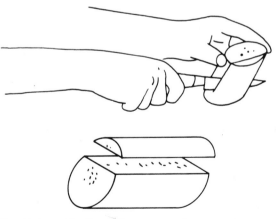

2. Cut a strip from the cucumber, as shown.

3. Holding the strip flat side down, make a series of diagonal slices across its length. These slices should be fairly close together for a graceful look. Leave a spine of about ½ inch to hold the slices together. Soak the strip in a salt solution (1 tablespoon salt, 1 quart water) for 10 minutes. Rinse.

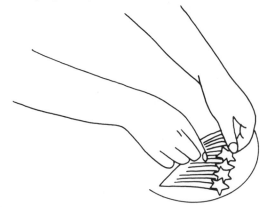

5. Using a star-shaped cutter (see Tools, page 2), punch out the stars.

4. Cut a carrot into ⅛-inch slices.

6. Place the cucumber on the serving plate and spread out the slices. Insert the stars between the cucumber slices.

EGG FROG

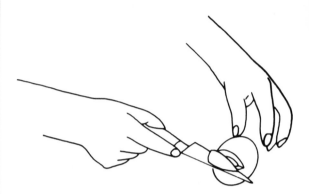

1. Cut a pie-shaped wedge from a peeled, hard-boiled egg for the mouth. You should also cut a flat slice off the bottom of the egg so it will sit upright.

2. Eyes can be made by cutting slits and inserting raisin halves. You can stop right here if you like. But if you want to go on, don't insert the eyes until you make the hat.

Here is a garnish for kids. To boil the egg, place it in cold water and slowly bring the water to a boil, uncovered. When the water boils, remove the pot from the heat and let it stand for 20 minutes. (This method will prevent overcooking, which may produce a green line between the yolk and the white.) Crack the egg and soak it in cold water for 6 minutes before peeling.

SERVING SUGGESTIONS: Use at children's (or adults') birthday parties or at picnics.

YOU WILL NEED: hard-boiled egg, carrot, raisins, vegetable peeler, paring knife, toothpick.

40

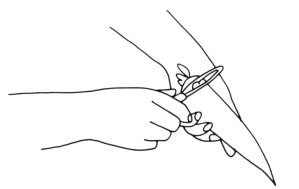

3. To make the hat, first peel a raw carrot.

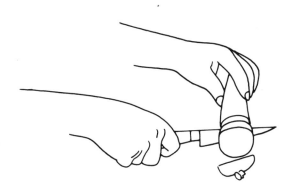

4. Cut two slices from the carrot, as shown. Cut one from the small end, the other from the big end.

5. These will become the brim and the crown of the hat, respectively, and can be pinned together and attached to the egg with a toothpick.

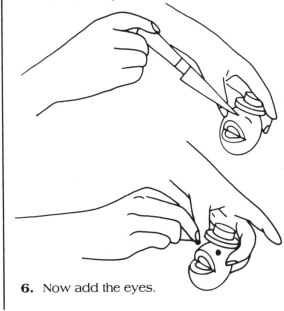

6. Now add the eyes.

41

EGG RABBIT

Naturally, no collection of egg garnishes would be complete without an Easter bunny for the kids. This Egg Rabbit is as close as we can come.

SERVING SUGGESTIONS: Use at Easter Sunday brunch or at children's birthday parties. Place a few Egg Rabbits in a nest of parsley or alfalfa sprouts. Or, put one in the children's lunch box.

YOU WILL NEED: hard-boiled egg, celery stalk, raisins, paring knife.

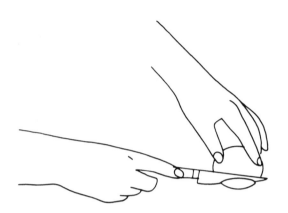

1. Cut a flat slice off the base of the egg so the rabbit will rest upright.

2. Cut two 2½-inch sections from a celery stalk.

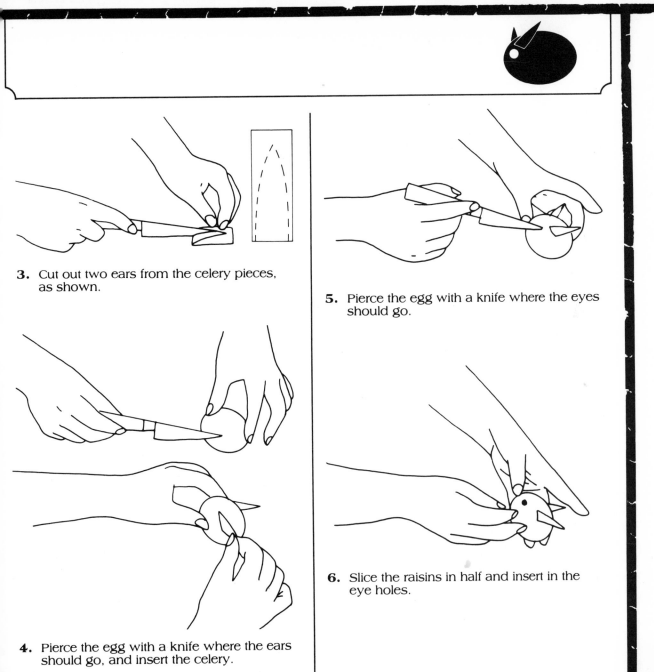

3. Cut out two ears from the celery pieces, as shown.

4. Pierce the egg with a knife where the ears should go, and insert the celery.

5. Pierce the egg with a knife where the eyes should go.

6. Slice the raisins in half and insert in the eye holes.

EGG CHICKEN

This one is for the kids, too. The carrots should be at room temperature. They are easier to cut when they are not cold and brittle. (See Egg Frog, page 40, for some helpful hints on boiling and peeling eggs.)

SERVING SUGGESTIONS: Egg Chickens are great for birthday parties, and they make a delightful surprise in a lunch box.

YOU WILL NEED: hard-boiled egg, carrot, paring knife, garnish knife.

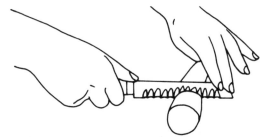

1. Using a garnish knife, cut a 2-inch section from a carrot. The garnish knife has a zigzag blade that is ideal for this kind of ribbed design (see Tools, page 2).

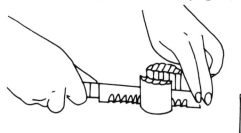

2. Still using the garnish knife, cut a piece from the center of the carrot section as shown. We are making a flat, ribbed piece of carrot which will be used for the tail.

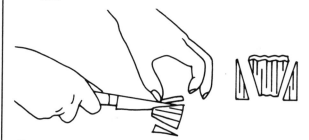

3. Now use a paring knife to cut the sides from this piece at an angle, as shown.

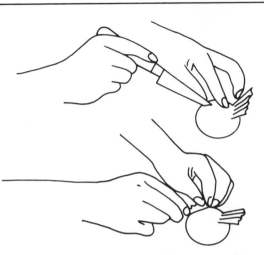

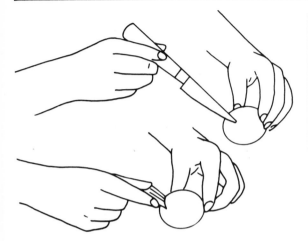

4. Make a slit near one end of a peeled, hard-boiled egg, and insert the tail. Also cut a flat slice off the bottom so the egg will sit upright.

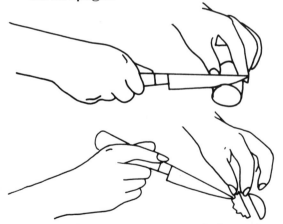

5. Cut another slice of carrot with the paring knife. Cut the slice in half and then fashion the comb by making zigzag cuts, as shown.

6. Make a slit in the top of the egg and insert the comb.

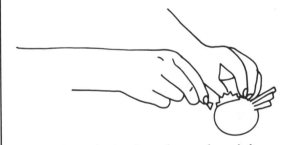

7. Fashion the beak and eyes from leftover pieces of carrot, and insert them into slits in the egg.

SQUARE EGG

The Square Egg became popular when kitchen supply stores began carrying the plastic mold that produces this curiosity. The mold is a clear plastic cube with a screw top device that forces the warm egg into the cube shape (see Tools, page 2). We think it's fun and are including it in case you've never encountered this unusual looking garnish.

SERVING SUGGESTIONS: Square Egg slices are especially eye-catching. Spread them fanwise next to a sandwich, or on a tray.

YOU WILL NEED: hard-boiled egg, square-egg mold, peppercorns or capers.

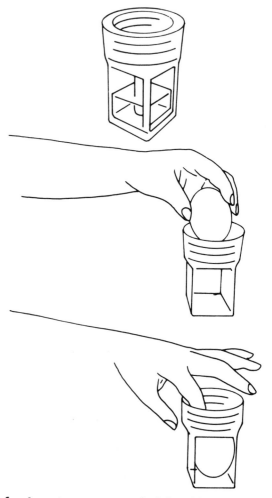

1. Insert a warm, peeled, hard-boiled egg into the mold. (Peeling the egg will be easier if, after boiling, you crack the shell in several places and then immerse the egg in cold water.)

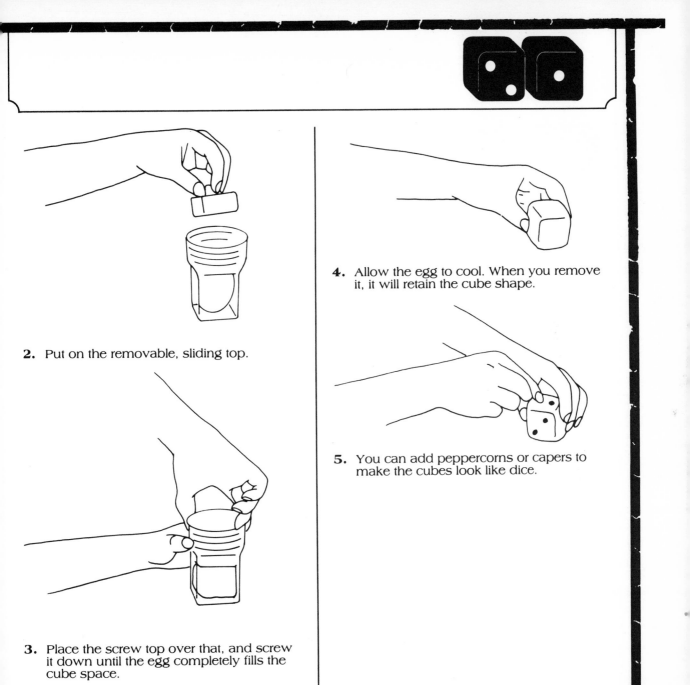

2. Put on the removable, sliding top.

3. Place the screw top over that, and screw it down until the egg completely fills the cube space.

4. Allow the egg to cool. When you remove it, it will retain the cube shape.

5. You can add peppercorns or capers to make the cubes look like dice.

EGG PINWHEEL

The Egg Pinwheel is a variation of the Square Egg (see page 46). Again, a warm egg is molded into a new shape. In this case, the molding is done with the hands.

SERVING SUGGESTIONS: The Egg Pinwheel can decorate the center of a platter of cold cuts or sandwiches.

YOU WILL NEED: hard-boiled egg, carrot, paring knife, chopstick.

1. Peel a hard-boiled egg while it is still warm. Place the warm egg in the palm of your hand, pointed end up.

2. With the other hand, gently flatten the egg into your palm. Be careful—too much pressure will split the egg. Hold the egg in this position for about a minute to produce a round, flattened-out egg.

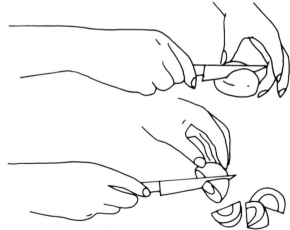

3. Cut the egg pancake into six wedges.

4. Arrange the wedges into a pinwheel shape.

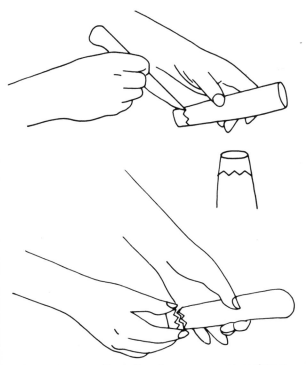

5. Cut a small section from a carrot, using a sawtooth cut (see Tomato Cups, page 72).

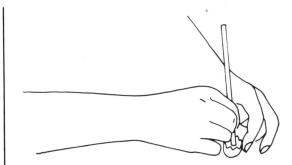

6. Punch out the center of the carrot slice with a chopstick.

7. Place the carrot in the center of the Egg Pinwheel.

ORANGE LOOPS

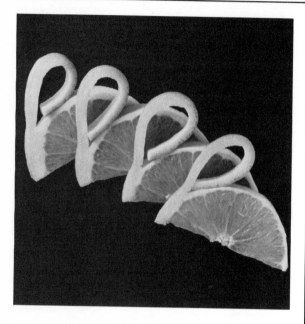

The Orange Loop is another favorite of ours. It shows how little work is required to create a pleasant design.

SERVING SUGGESTIONS: Orange Loops can be used to garnish duck à l'orange or as a garnish for pork. They also look attractive on a fruit salad or arranged around the rim of a tall fruit drink.

YOU WILL NEED: orange, paring knife.

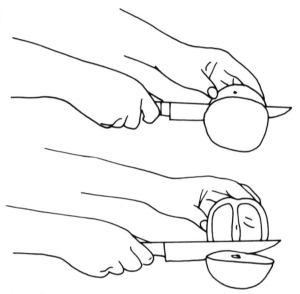

1. Slice an orange in half. The cut should be made through the stem as shown, not through the equator.

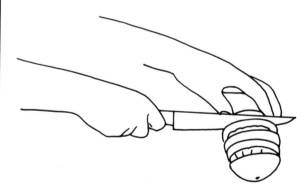

2. Cut the orange halves into slices about ⅜ inch thick.

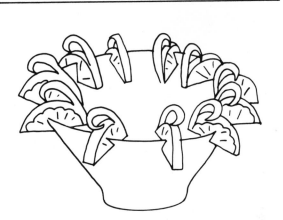

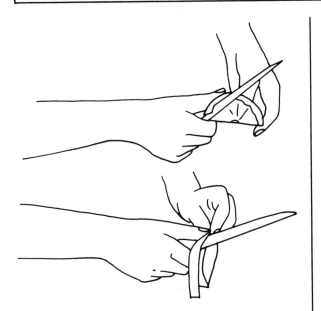

3. Make a cut between the skin and the orange to separate the skin. Cut almost to the end, leaving only about 1 inch of skin connected.

5. Orange Loops can be slit and arranged around the rim of a punchbowl, as shown.

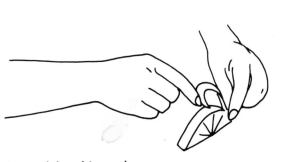

4. Curl the skin under.

ORANGE STAR

The Orange Star is a very familiar, often used, and always useful garnish. This simple and decorative cut can also be used for grapefruits, lemons, or tomatoes.

SERVING SUGGESTIONS: The Orange Star can be used to garnish a plate of cold cuts, a duck à l'orange, or a cheese tray. A Lemon Star can be served with poached fish or baked chicken.

YOU WILL NEED: orange, paring knife.

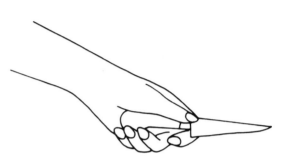

1. Select a small, sharp paring knife with a blade no wider than ¾ inch.

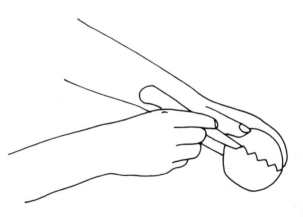

2. Insert the knife at the equator of the orange and penetrate through to the center. This should be a diagonal cut. Continue alternating this diagonal cut completely around the orange in a sawtooth fashion.

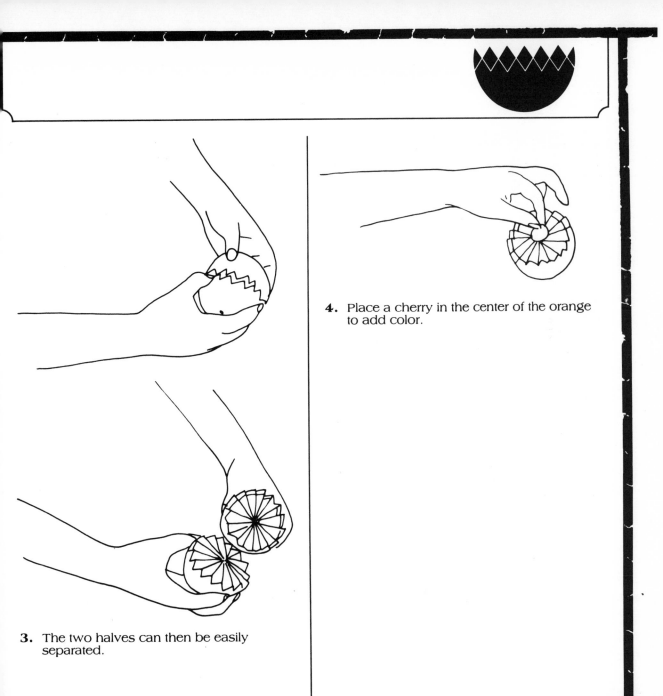

4. Place a cherry in the center of the orange to add color.

3. The two halves can then be easily separated.

RADISH BUDS

The radish is a member of the mustard family. It has a pungent root that can be eaten raw. The small red Cherry Belle or Comet radish has been the raw material for numerous garnish designs. Most variations, like the Radish Bud, depend on carving it up in different ways.

SERVING SUGGESTIONS: Radish Buds can be used with a cucumber salad, a chicory and dill salad, or a beef salad.

YOU WILL NEED: radish, paring knife, bowl of ice water.

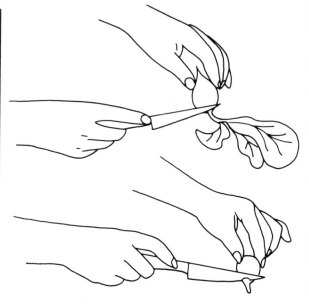

1. Cut the leaves and tip from a radish.

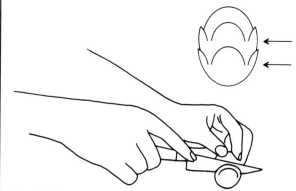

2. Make two cuts in each of the four sides of the radish. The tip end of the radish should be up.

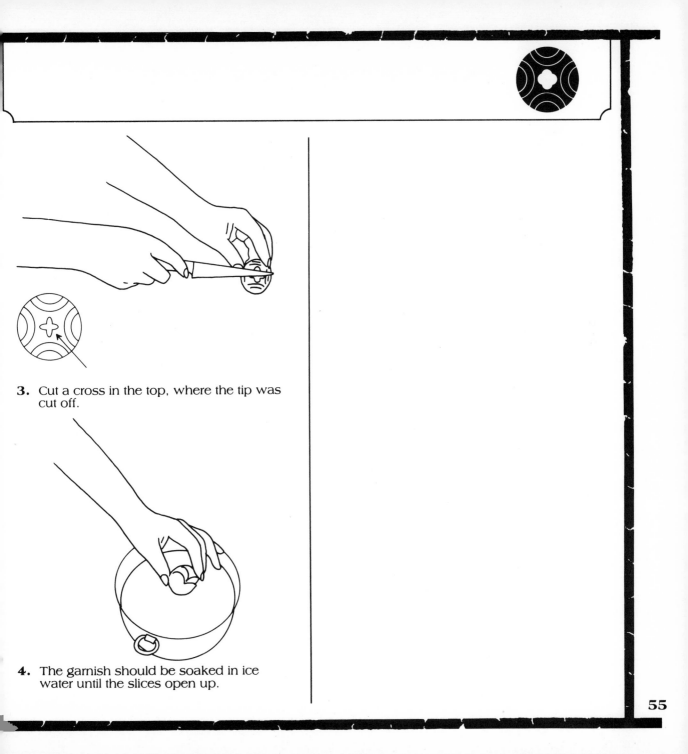

3. Cut a cross in the top, where the tip was cut off.

4. The garnish should be soaked in ice water until the slices open up.

RADISH MUSHROOMS

1. Cut away the leaves and tip of a radish.

Another easy way to carve radishes is to turn them into little mushrooms. Drop them onto a nest of alfalfa sprouts for a nice garnish, and add an Egg Chicken (page 44) for fun.

SERVING SUGGESTIONS: Radish Mushrooms can be used as hors d'oeuvres with a dip, in an alfalfa sprout salad, or in a mushroom salad.

YOU WILL NEED: radish, paring knife.

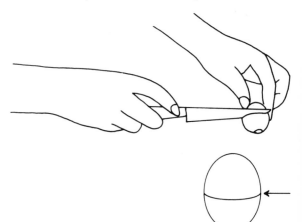

2. Cut a line about ¼ inch deep completely around the center of the radish.

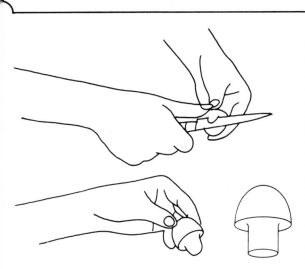

3. Shape the stem by cutting from the base (leaf end) to the center cut, as shown.

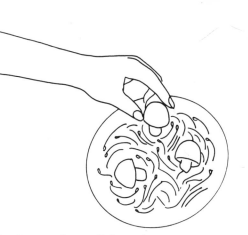

5. Scatter the radishes about.

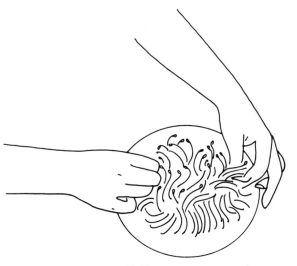

4. Arrange some alfalfa sprouts on a plate.

RADISH FAN

The effectiveness of this garnish will depend upon how well you can cut the radish into a multitude of thin slices. For best results, use a small, sharp knife with a fairly thin blade.

SERVING SUGGESTIONS: Arrange Radish Fans around the edge of a platter of cold cuts, place on top of an open-face egg salad sandwich, or use to surround a mound of chicken salad.

YOU WILL NEED: radish, paring knife.

1. Pick out a radish with nice leaves. The leaves will stay on as part of the finished garnish.

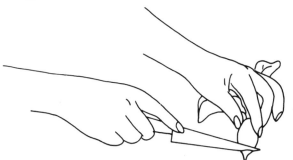

2. Cut off the tip.

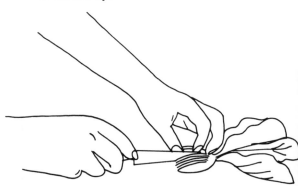

3. Cut the radish, making as many thin slices as you can.

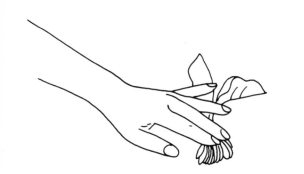

4. Spread out the radish in a fanlike manner. The radish will be easier to spread if soaked in a salt solution (1 tablespoon salt, 1 quart water) for a few minutes. Be sure the leaves don't touch the salt water; if they do, they'll wilt. Rinse.

RADISH JACKS

When it comes to Radish Jacks, the rule is: The more the merrier. Make as many of these jacks as you can. Fortunately, they are fast and easy to do.

SERVING SUGGESTIONS: Sprinkle on a tuna or Caesar salad. Stand one or two up on deviled-egg halves.

YOU WILL NEED: radish, paring knife.

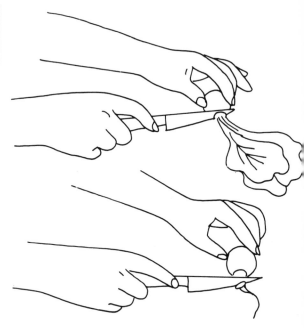

1. Cut the leaves and tip from a radish.

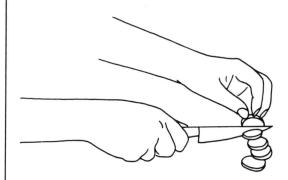

2. Cut the radish into ⅛-inch slices.

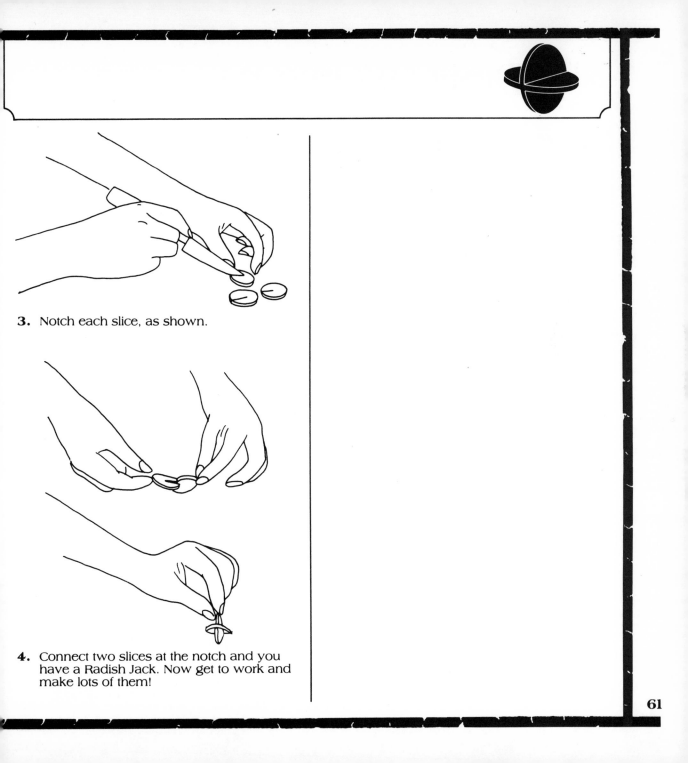

3. Notch each slice, as shown.

4. Connect two slices at the notch and you have a Radish Jack. Now get to work and make lots of them!

RADISH BLOSSOM

Up to this point we have been using the small red Cherry Belle or Comet radishes. The Radish Blossom requires the big, white Oriental radish known as the Japanese Daikon, which can grow up to several feet in length. It is available in Oriental food stores and large supermarkets.

SERVING SUGGESTIONS: The Radish Blossom will make a beautiful centerpiece for any serving platter.

YOU WILL NEED: Daikon, yellow squash, Japanese chef's knife, vegetable peeler, V-shaped chisel, toothpick, bowl of ice water.

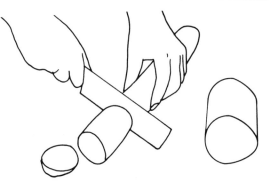

1. Cut a 4-inch section from a Daikon. Peel. Form into a slight heart shape, as shown.

2. Cut five grooves down one side about ½ inch apart, as shown. These grooves can be cut with an ordinary knife or, if you have one, a wood chisel with a V-tipped blade.

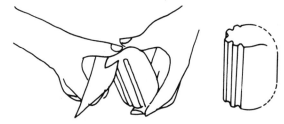

3. Shape the radish as shown. The ends should be rounded slightly.

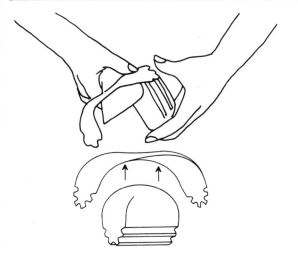

4. The petals can be made from this shaped radish by cutting a slice lengthwise around both ends. Succeeding cuts can be made to get more petals. The petals will get smaller as the radish gets smaller. Soak the petals in ice cold water to make them curl.

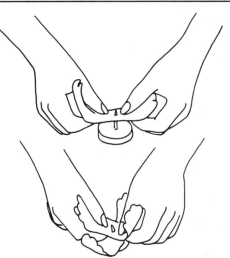

6. Stick the petals on this toothpick at right angles to each other, beginning with the largest and ending with the smallest.

5. Make a base for the flower by cutting a section from the radish and inserting a toothpick.

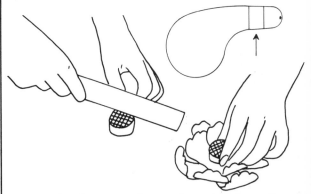

7. Make the center by cutting a 1-inch section from the neck of a yellow squash. This piece should be scored in a crisscross fashion and stuck onto the toothpick.

RADISH NET

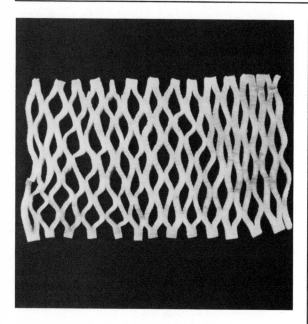

The Radish Net is a difficult garnish to make. It takes a skilled Mukimono chef to accomplish the continuous peeling cut that is required. But it is so traditional that we feel the book wouldn't be complete without it. As in the Radish Blossom (page 62), we use the large Japanese Daikon instead of the small, round radishes.

SERVING SUGGESTIONS: Place over steamed mussels or on a boiled lobster half.

YOU WILL NEED: Daikon, Japanese chef's knife, skewer, bowl of salt solution.

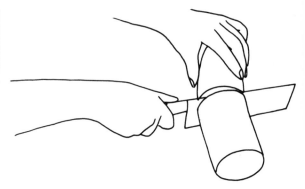

1. Use a Japanese chef's knife to cut a 4-inch section from the Daikon. The radish should be smooth and soft to the touch.

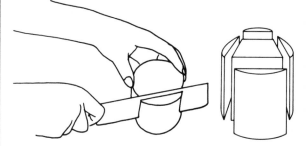

2. Remove the four sides, leaving a block.

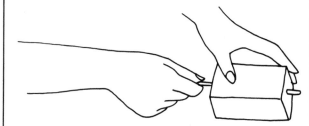

3. Insert a skewer through the center of the block.

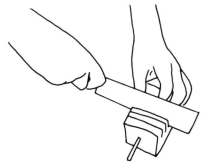

4. Make straight cuts down to the skewer on all four sides. Space the cuts about ½ inch apart. Start with the top side.

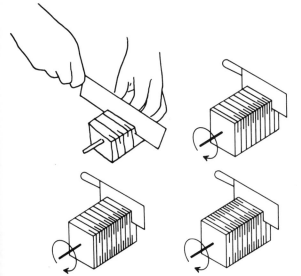

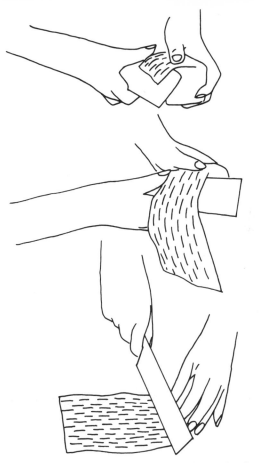

5. Then turn the block away from you and make the second side cuts between the first as shown. Continue to go around the block in this way until all four sides have been sliced.

6. So far so good, but now comes the hard part. Using your broad knife, peel the radish into one long rectangular strip. (See steps 3 and 4 in Carrot Curls, page 14.) This strip should be soaked in salt solution (1 tablespoon salt, 1 quart water) for 5 minutes to soften the radish so it will open up into a nicely defined net. Rinse.

TOMATO BUTTERFLY

We have Mexico to thank for the tomato. It was cultivated by the Indians for centuries and known as *tomatl*. For some reason, the tomato didn't become a significant commercial crop in America until the 1880s. Of course now, along with lettuce and potatoes, it is one of the top three vegetable sellers.

SERVING SUGGESTIONS: We have put two wedges together to resemble a butterfly. Of course, the wedges can also be used separately. You might use them on a platter of poached fish, or in a salad.

YOU WILL NEED: tomato, paring knife.

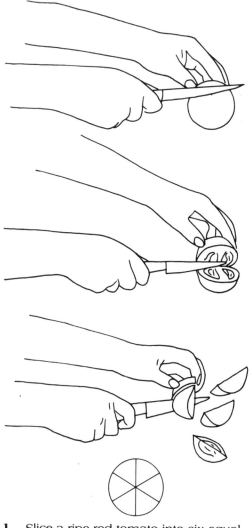

1. Slice a ripe red tomato into six equal wedges.

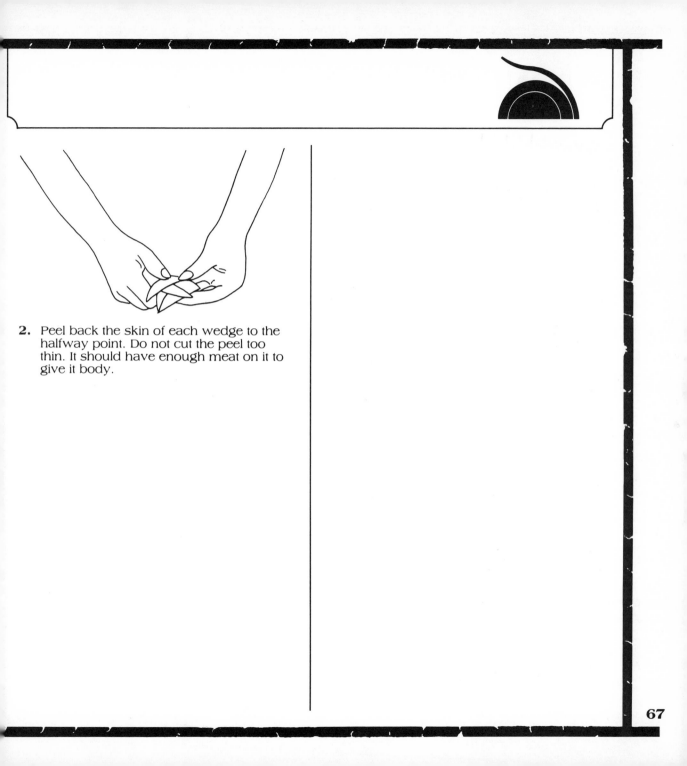

2. Peel back the skin of each wedge to the halfway point. Do not cut the peel too thin. It should have enough meat on it to give it body.

TOMATO CAMELIA

The Tomato Camelia is a favorite with us because it exemplifies simplicity—the quality upon which all good Mukimono depends.

SERVING SUGGESTIONS: Leaves from the garden can be added to the Tomato Camelia. It can also be used with Tomato Tulips (see page 70) to create a larger, more decorative garnish appropriate for the center of a large serving platter.

YOU WILL NEED: tomato, paring knife.

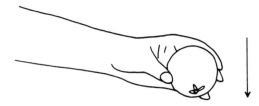

1. Select a medium-size tomato and place it stem-end down on the cutting board.

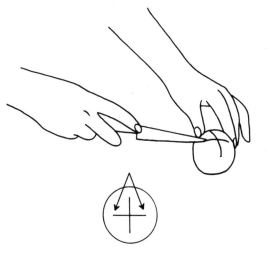

2. Make two cuts at right angles to each other across the top. The cuts should be about 2 inches long and just deep enough to barely pierce the skin.

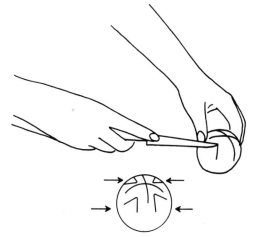

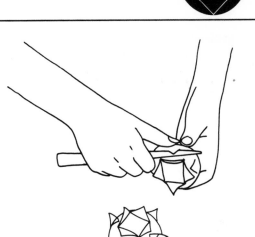

3. Now make four right-angle cuts below these, as shown. These are for the lower petals.

5. Complete the garnish by peeling back the lower petals.

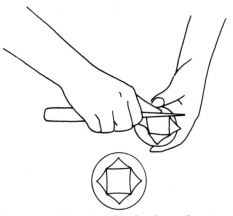

4. Now peel the skin back along the top cuts to form the flower. Try to keep the skin from becoming too thin when you peel it, or it will shrivel up.

TOMATO TULIP

The Tomato Tulip is similar to the Tomato Camelia (page 68), but it is done with cherry tomatoes that are usually about an inch or so in diameter. Although cherry tomatoes can be grown in most parts of the United States, California and Mexico are the major suppliers.

SERVING SUGGESTIONS: Use on top of a bowl of tossed salad. Use as a garnish for broiled chops or steak, or on a toothpick atop a club sandwich.

YOU WILL NEED: cherry tomato, paring knife.

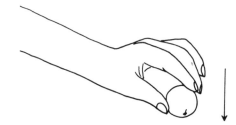

1. Select a nice, plump cherry tomato and place it on your cutting board, stem-end down.

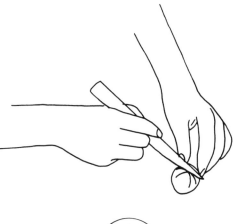

2. Make three cuts across the top, as shown. These cuts should just barely pierce the skin. Be careful not to cut too deeply into the meat.

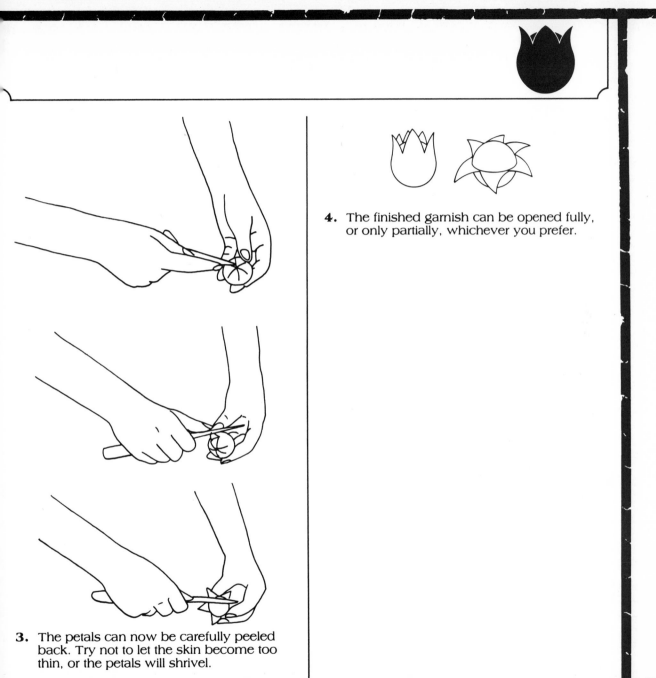

4. The finished garnish can be opened fully, or only partially, whichever you prefer.

3. The petals can now be carefully peeled back. Try not to let the skin become too thin, or the petals will shrivel.

TOMATO CUPS

The sawtooth cut is one that you are probably familiar with by now (see Orange Star, page 52). It is a decorative cut that is used quite often to slice many different fruits in half. In the case of the Tomato Cup, it is carried one step further. By hollowing out each half, you create a cup that can be used to hold food.

SERVING SUGGESTIONS: Fill with shrimp, potato salad, tuna salad, etc. Or fill with peas and serve with a roast.

YOU WILL NEED: tomato, paring knife, spoon.

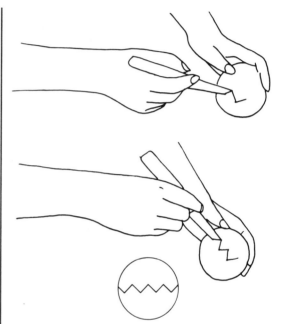

1. Make a sawtooth cut around the circumference of a tomato. The knife blade should penetrate to the center.

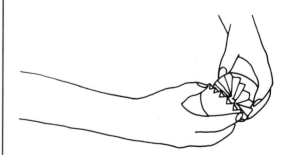

2. Once the cut is completed, the tomato can be easily separated into halves.

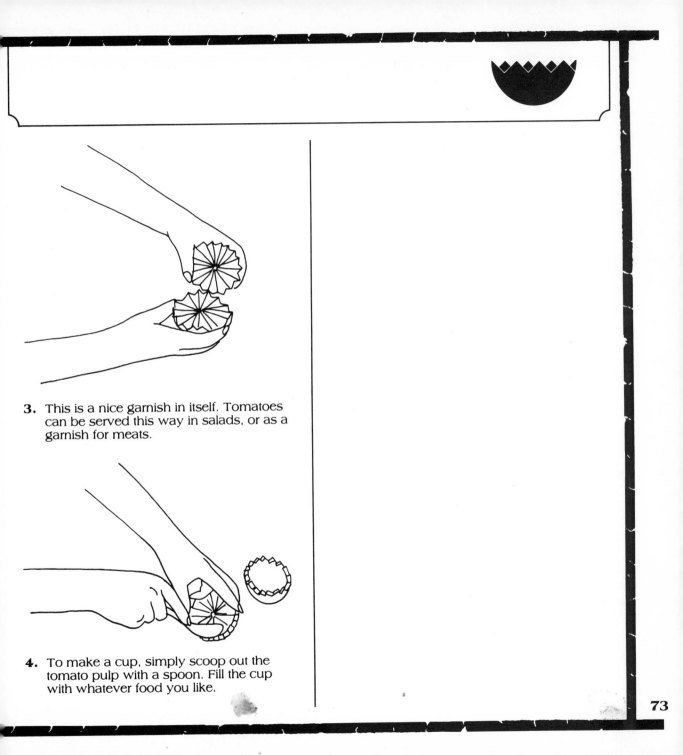

3. This is a nice garnish in itself. Tomatoes can be served this way in salads, or as a garnish for meats.

4. To make a cup, simply scoop out the tomato pulp with a spoon. Fill the cup with whatever food you like.

TOMATO ROSE

The Tomato Rose is a popular garnish. We believe its origin is European rather than Japanese. Although it looks complicated, it is really one of the simplest garnishes to make.

SERVING SUGGESTIONS: The Tomato Rose has been used to garnish just about everything. It has probably appeared at more restaurant buffets than potato salad. Try it with a platter of fish quenelles in a white sauce for color contrast.

YOU WILL NEED: tomato, paring knife, lettuce leaves.

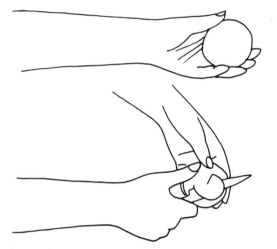

1. Select a firm tomato and begin to peel it in a long strip. The strip should be about ½ inch wide. A small, sharp paring knife will do the job.

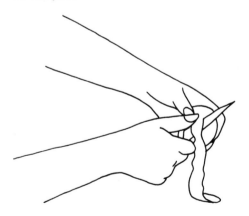

2. Try to peel the entire tomato in one long continuous strip.

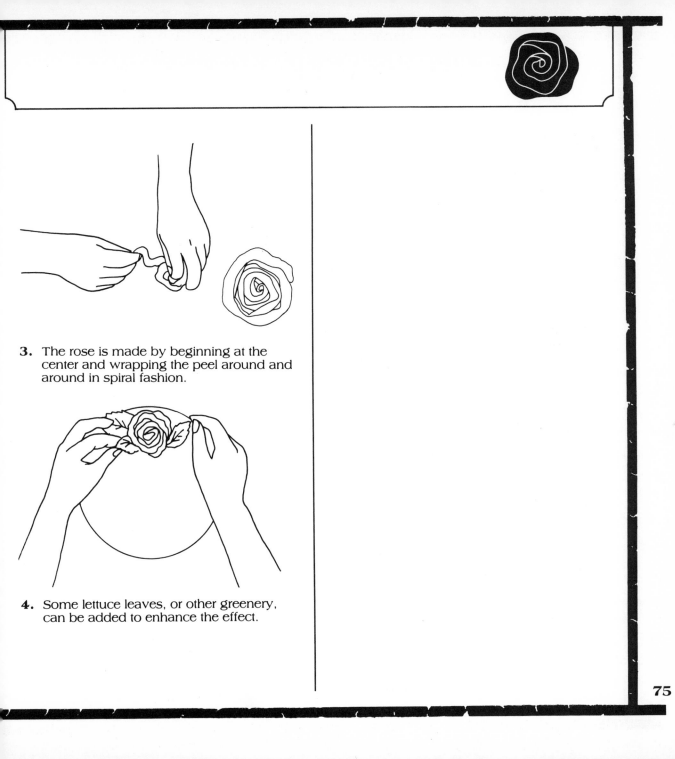

3. The rose is made by beginning at the center and wrapping the peel around and around in spiral fashion.

4. Some lettuce leaves, or other greenery, can be added to enhance the effect.

TOMATO ARTICHOKE

The Tomato Artichoke uses only the tomato peel rather than the whole tomato. The peel from six tomato wedges is simply reassembled in the shape of an artichoke.

SERVING SUGGESTIONS: Use a Tomato Artichoke at each end of an oval serving plate. Leaves from the garden can be added under the garnish. Place it on a platter of open-face sandwiches or stuffed green peppers.

YOU WILL NEED: tomato, paring knife.

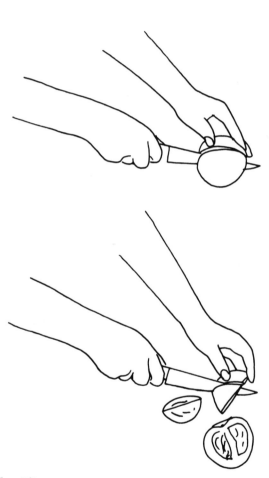

1. Slice a tomato into six equal wedges.

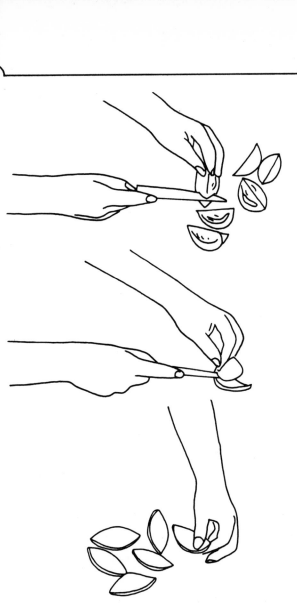

3. Assemble the six peels on the serving plate in the order shown in the diagram.

2. Most of the meat should be sliced away from the peel, but leave enough meat for body.

TURNIP BLOSSOM

Turnips have been cultivated since ancient times. They are said to have had their origins in Russia and Scandinavia, but now, of course, they are found all over the world. Turnips are available all year round, but they are especially abundant in the fall and winter. So, during those months when fruits and other vegetables are hard to come by, we can turn to the turnip for our raw material.

SERVING SUGGESTIONS: Cook until just done and place in tomato aspic.

YOU WILL NEED: turnip, piece of carrot, paring knife, skewer, plastic straw or chopstick.

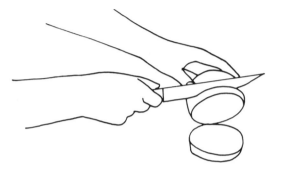

1. Cut a ½-inch-thick slice from an unpeeled white turnip.

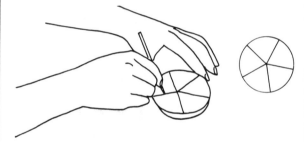

2. Using a skewer, score five equally spaced lines on the face of the slice.

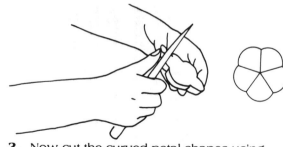

3. Now cut the curved petal shapes using these lines as a guide.

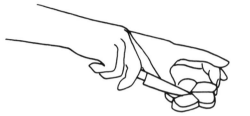

4. Slice about ¼ inch into the turnip along each of the guidelines.

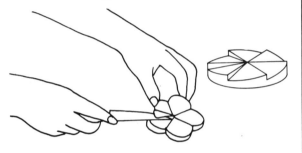

5. Remove a wedge from each petal by making an angle cut to the bottom of each guideline.

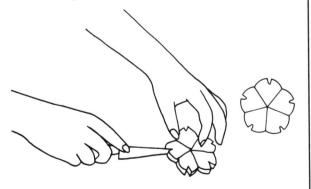

6. Cut a notch in the middle of each petal.

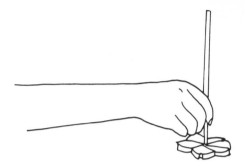

7. Punch out the center with a plastic straw or chopstick.

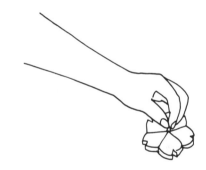

8. Place a little piece of carrot in the center.

TURNIP CHICKS

Turnip Chicks, like Carrot Spurs and Carrot Corn, use a technique that comes close to mass production. It involves carving the whole turnip into the shape desired, and then slicing that shape into many garnishes.

SERVING SUGGESTIONS: Turnip Chicks can be added to a green salad or a homemade vegetable soup. They can be served hot, boiled until just done and seasoned with butter, salt, and pepper.

YOU WILL NEED: turnip, paring knife, vegetable peeler, skewer, Japanese chef's knife.

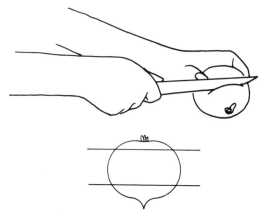

1. Cut the top and bottom from a turnip.

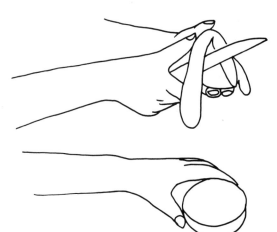

2. Peel with either a knife or a vegetable peeler. We are trying to create a cylinder, so even up the sides as much as possible.

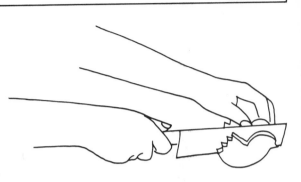

3. Using a skewer, carve the chick design into the face of the turnip.

6. Slice the turnip to create many little chicks.

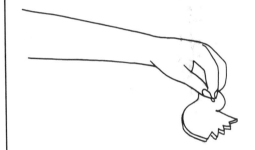

4. Cut away the excess turnip around that shape.

7. If you like, capers or peppercorns can be used for eyes.

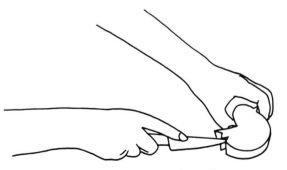

5. Cut a notched design in the tail.

TURNIP NETTLES

To make Turnip Nettles, use just the stem of a beet or turnip. Turnip greens are usually cooked like spinach or other greens. We are using the stems raw; but don't worry, they are delicious.

SERVING SUGGESTIONS: Use with a tomato salad or a mixed green salad. Or make a nest for an Egg Frog or Egg Chicken (see pages 40, 44).

YOU WILL NEED: turnip or beet leaves, paring knife, bowl of ice water.

1. Cut the stems from a turnip or beet.

2. Cut the leaves away from the stem.

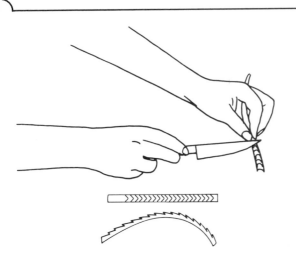

3. Make a series of angled cuts down the length of the stem.

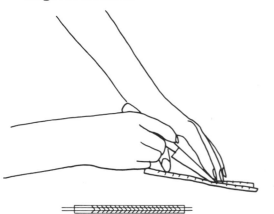

4. This stem should then be cut lengthwise into thin strips—the thinner the better, as they will curl more easily. You should be able to get at least three strips out of a stem.

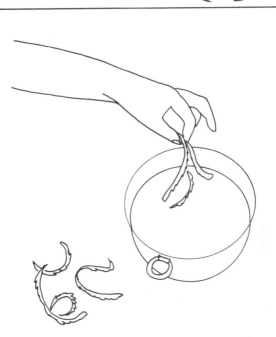

5. Drop the strips into ice cold water. This will cause them to curl up tightly.

TURNIP MUM

The Turnip Mum is an impressive garnish. It is large enough to be used as the centerpiece on a large serving platter. Its effect can be further enhanced, as we have done, by dyeing it with food coloring and adding leaves from the garden.

SERVING SUGGESTIONS: Use as a centerpiece for a platter of cold meats or on a platter of pate. Or use in the center of a platter of fresh vegetables with dip.

YOU WILL NEED: turnip, paring knife, two chopsticks, bowl of salt solution, bowl of food-coloring solution.

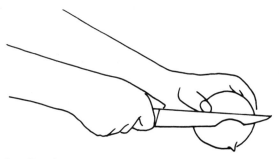

1. Cut the stem and tip off a large turnip.

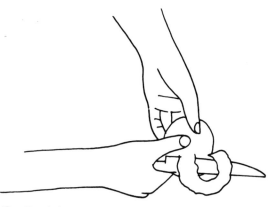

2. Peel the turnip completely.

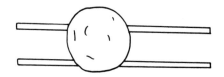

3. Place the turnip between two chopsticks on the cutting board.

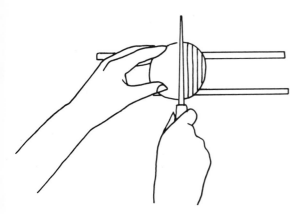

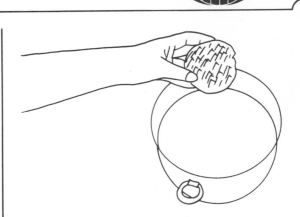

4. Make a series of slices down to the chopsticks. The chopsticks will prevent the knife from cutting all of the way through the turnip. These slices should be about ⅛ inch apart.

6. Soak the turnip in a salt solution (1 tablespoon salt, 1 quart water) for at least 10 minutes. This will cause the slices to open up. Rinse.

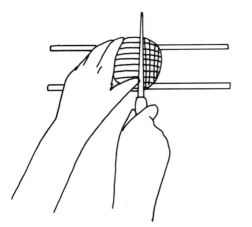

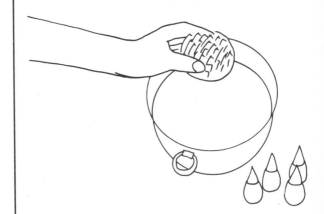

5. Turn the turnip 90 degrees and make another series of cuts at right angles to the first.

7. For color, soak the garnish in a solution of food coloring.

SQUASH FEATHER

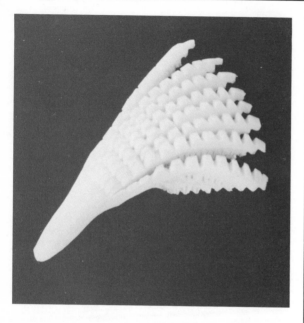

The Squash Feather uses the method of notching a design into the skin of a vegetable and then slicing it into many leaves. This technique is much admired and used quite often in Mukimono.

SERVING SUGGESTIONS: Place around a platter of chicken salad in Tomato Cups (see page 72), or make a wreath with parsley around oysters in molded aspic.

YOU WILL NEED: yellow squash, paring knife, garnish knife, bowl of salt solution.

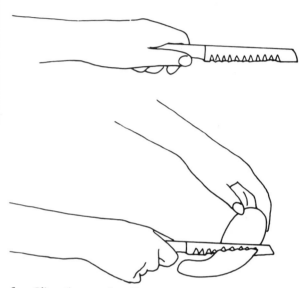

1. Slice the neck off a yellow squash, using a garnish knife.

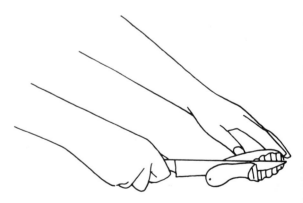

2. Then, with a paring knife, cut off the inner curve of the neck to produce a flat base.

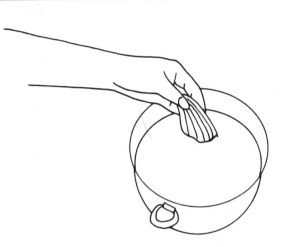

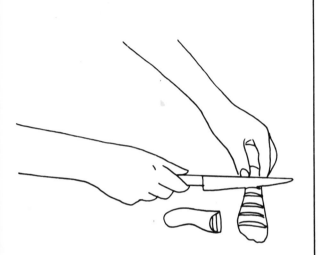

3. With the squash neck flat side down, make a series of notches in the skin to about 1 inch of the small end.

5. Soak in a salt solution (1 tablespoon salt, 1 quart water) until it is soft enough to spread open with the fingers, about 5 minutes. Rinse.

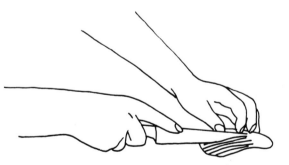

4. Make lengthwise slices, also to about 1 inch from the end.

ZUCCHINI PALM

Squash has been growing in the Americas for close to five thousand years. The popular zucchini named by the Italians is best when it is small to medium in size.

SERVING SUGGESTIONS: Arrange around Tomato Cups (see page 72) stuffed with chicken salad, or marinate in sweet and sour marinade and place around deep-fried fish.

YOU WILL NEED: zucchini, paring knife, bowl of salt solution.

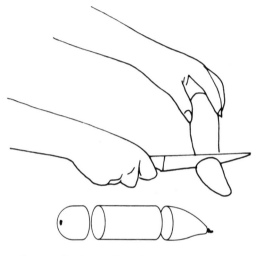

1. Cut a 4-inch section from an unpeeled zucchini.

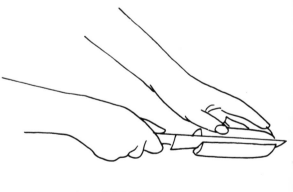

2. Cut that section in half, lengthwise.

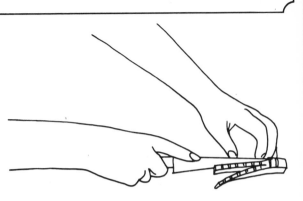

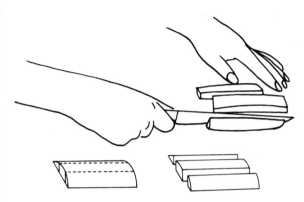

3. Lay one of the halves flat on the cutting board. Cut away the two sides, leaving a flat piece about ¾ inch wide and 4 inches long.

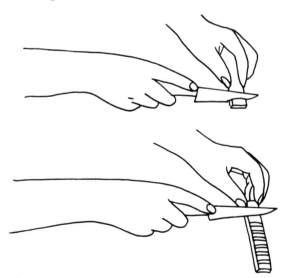

4. Cut notches along the top of this piece, as shown, to about 1 inch from the end.

5. Make five lengthwise slits, also to about 1 inch from the end.

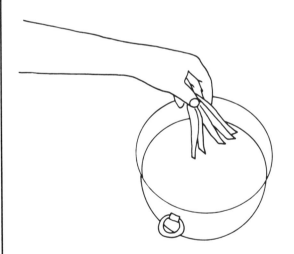

6. This forms the leaves. Soaked in a salt solution (1 tablespoon salt, 1 quart water) for ten minutes, the leaves will soften and open easily when spread with the fingers. Rinse.

ZUCCHINI DAISY

Zucchini, or soft-shelled squash, is always available, although the supply is at its best from June through August. The Zucchini Daisy is another application of the sawtooth cut that we have used for the Orange Star and Tomato Cup.

SERVING SUGGESTIONS: Cook in boiling water until just done, and season with butter, salt, and pepper. Serve it as a vegetable dish. Uncooked, serve with other green vegetables for a dip.

YOU WILL NEED: zucchini, piece of carrot, paring knife, chopstick or plastic straw.

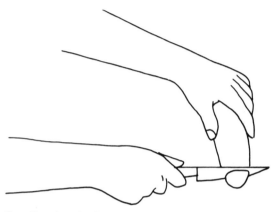

1. Cut the tip from a zucchini.

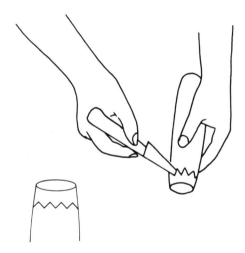

2. With a small-bladed knife, make a sawtooth cut around the circumference of the zucchini about 1 inch up from the bottom. This is done by inserting the knife to the center at alternating angles (see Orange Star, page 52).

3. The garnish can be easily removed.

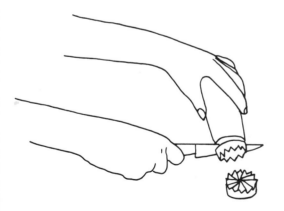

4. Additional garnishes can be cut from the zucchini.

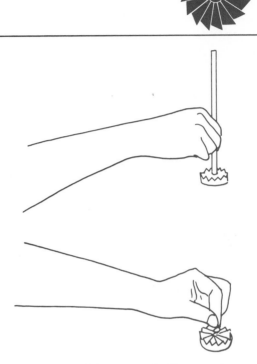

5. Because of the many knife cuts, the center of the garnish may not be attractive. Often this center is punched out with a chopstick or plastic straw and a small piece of carrot added for color.

MELON FANS

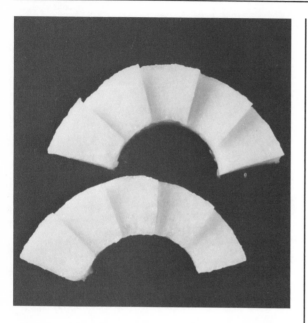

Melons originated in the Near East and then spread to Europe. It is thought that Christopher Columbus planted the first melons in the New World. The cantaloupe is probably the most popular of the sweet melons, and the Melon Fan is a popular garnish.

SERVING SUGGESTIONS: Use in a mixed fruit compote or arrange Melon Fans with some slices of prosciutto for an appetizer.

YOU WILL NEED: cantaloupe, paring knife, small measuring cup.

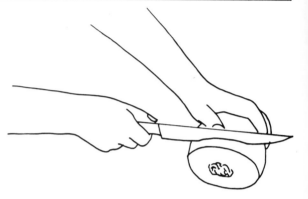

1. Slice a cantaloupe into 1-inch-thick rounds.

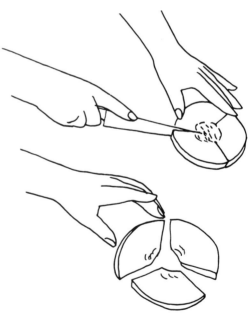

2. Cut the melon rounds into thirds.

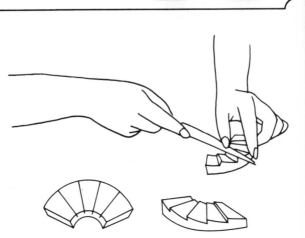

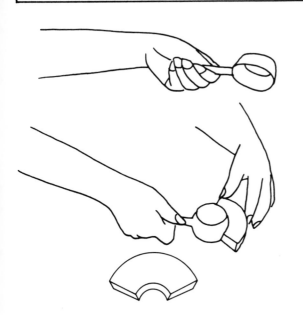

3. Cut away the seeds in the center with any curved object, such as a measuring cup.

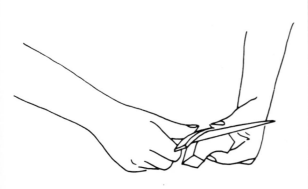

4. Cut away the skin. This produces the basic fan shape.

5. The fan pattern is created by making four or five radiating cuts on the face of the melon about ¼ inch deep. Slanting cuts are then made and the wedges removed.

MAPLE LEAF

The Japanese delight in nature, and Mukimono is often an expression of that feeling. In this case, little Maple Leaves are created from a beet.

SERVING SUGGESTIONS: Cook until just done, then season with sweet and sour sauce and serve as a vegetable dish. Try sprinkling them uncooked on a green salad. Or cook until just done in boiling salt water, then place on an omelet, around a meatloaf, or on a baked chicken.

YOU WILL NEED: beet, paring knife, skewer, V-shaped chisel.

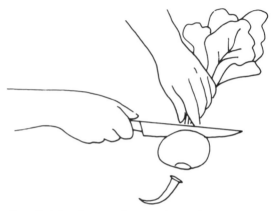

1. Cut the leaves from a large beet.

2. Slice off part of each end to create a cylindrical shape.

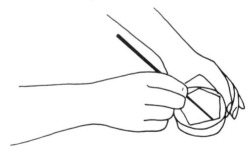

3. Score a pentagon on the face of one end with a metal skewer.

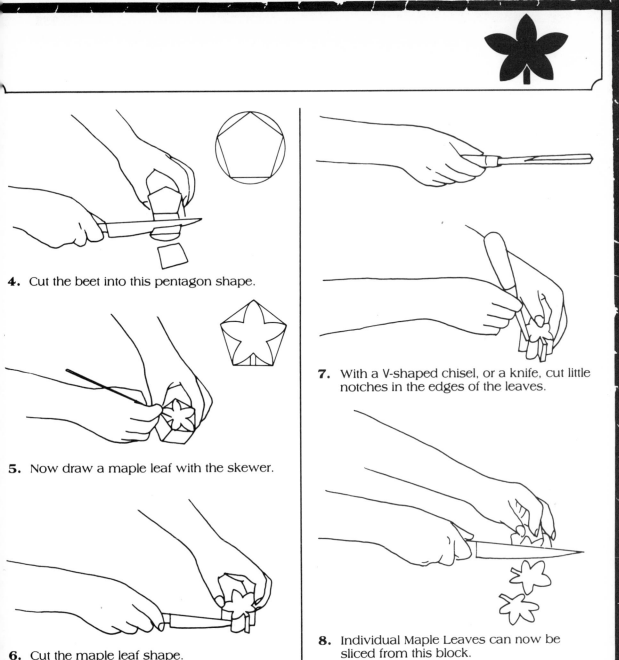

4. Cut the beet into this pentagon shape.

5. Now draw a maple leaf with the skewer.

6. Cut the maple leaf shape.

7. With a V-shaped chisel, or a knife, cut little notches in the edges of the leaves.

8. Individual Maple Leaves can now be sliced from this block.

ONION FLOWER

More Mukimono magic! Here's how to turn a lowly onion into a beautiful flower. It's done by slicing each layer of the onion into petal shapes. A sliced onion, even one on its way to becoming a flower, will still make you cry. The best solution is to refrigerate the onion before slicing. This will minimize the pungent fumes.

SERVING SUGGESTIONS: Make various size flowers and arrange as a centerpiece for a buffet.

YOU WILL NEED: large onion, paring knife, bowl of ice water.

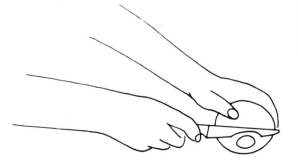

1. Slice off the base (stem end) of a large yellow onion.

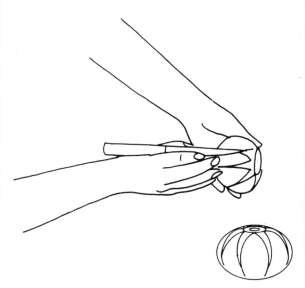

2. With a paring knife, cut the outer onion layer into petal shapes, as shown. Cut through only one layer, and leave petals connected at the bottom.

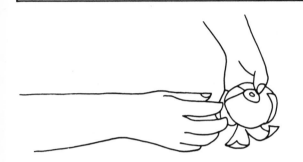

3. Open the petals so that the next onion layer is exposed.

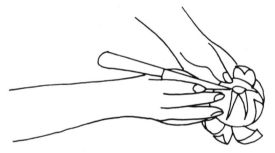

4. Slice this next layer into petal shapes. These petals should be cut so as to be offset from the first layer.

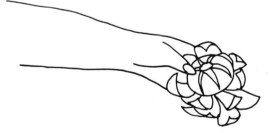

5. Open the petals and cut the next layer.

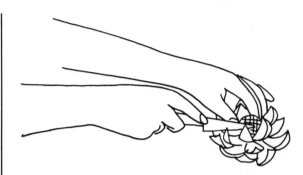

6. Continue in this manner for as many layers as possible. Using a crisscross pattern, slice up whatever onion remains in the center.

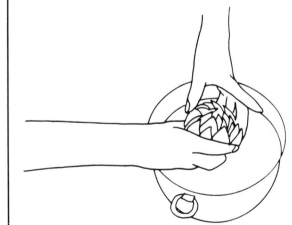

7. Soak the onion in ice water. This will cause the petals to open easily.

POTATO SPRING

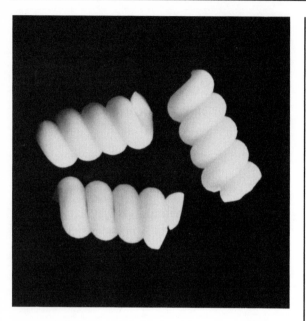

This is another one of those marvelous garnishes in which a mysterious looking tool easily produces an intricate, clever garnish. The potato cutter should be available in local kitchen supply shops. By all means get one. The results are delightful.

SERVING SUGGESTIONS: Potato Springs can be either fried or boiled and used to garnish just about any main course.

YOU WILL NEED: potato, paring knife, potato cutter.

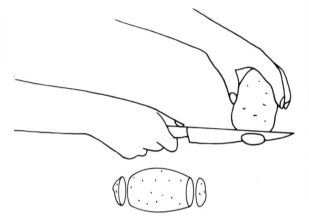

1. Cut the ends off a fairly small potato. It is not necessary to peel it.

2. The garnish is made with the potato cutter, which is held as shown (see Tools, page 2).

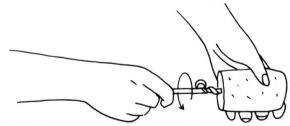

3. The tool is simply inserted into one end of the potato with a clockwise motion.

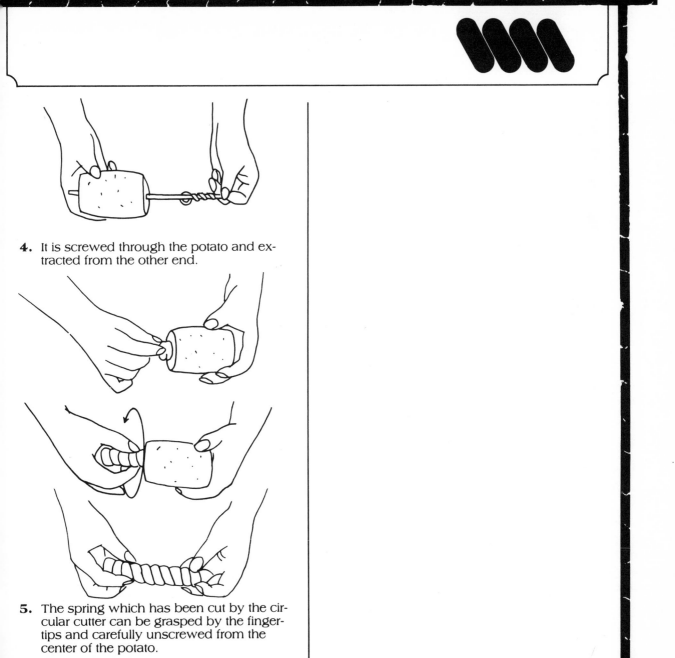

4. It is screwed through the potato and extracted from the other end.

5. The spring which has been cut by the circular cutter can be grasped by the fingertips and carefully unscrewed from the center of the potato.

SCALLION BRUSH

The Scallion Brush is a garnish that has been around for a long time. It needs no special tools, but the knife you use should be fairly small and thin-bladed.

SERVING SUGGESTIONS: Place a Scallion Brush on top of a serving of beef salad, or use several on a platter surrounding deep-fried oysters.

YOU WILL NEED: scallion, paring knife, bowl of ice water.

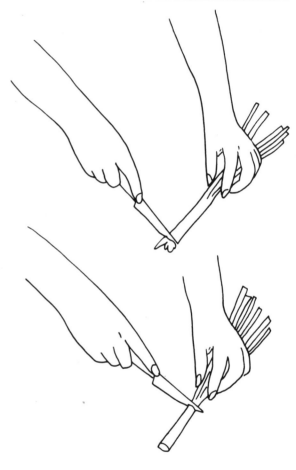

1. Cut a 3-inch section from the stem of a scallion. The tip should be removed.

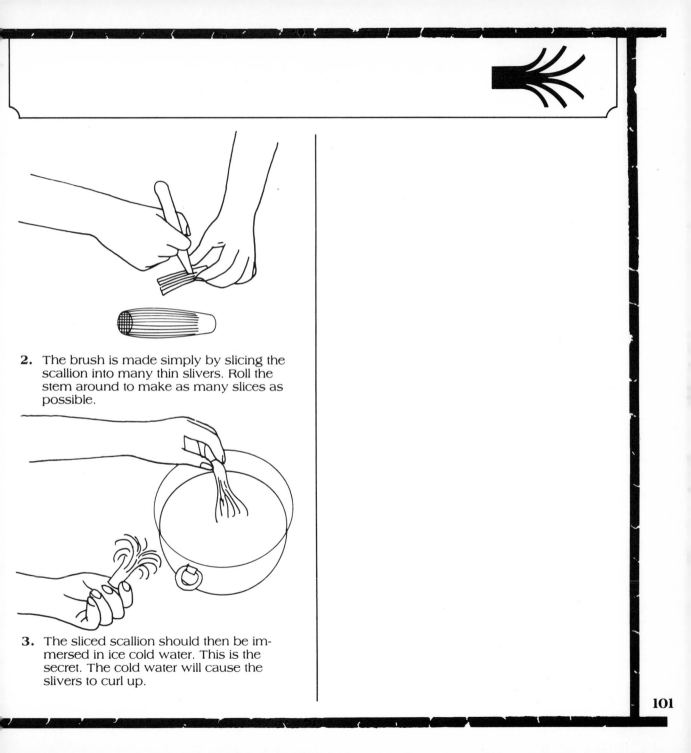

2. The brush is made simply by slicing the scallion into many thin slivers. Roll the stem around to make as many slices as possible.

3. The sliced scallion should then be immersed in ice cold water. This is the secret. The cold water will cause the slivers to curl up.

LOTUS PEACOCK

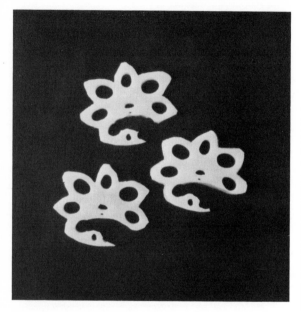

For the last garnish we have selected one where Mother Nature has done most of the work. The Lotus Peacock takes advantage of the curious hole pattern running through the lotus root. This is a crunchy, edible winter root available in Oriental markets.

SERVING SUGGESTIONS: Cook until just done in boiling salted water, then marinate in sweet and sour marinade. Serve around deep-fried fish filets, or use uncooked in vegetable soup.

YOU WILL NEED: lotus root, paring knife, vegetable peeler, skewer, bowl of Fruit-Fresh solution.

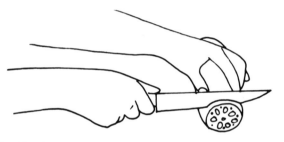

1. Peel a section of lotus root and cut several slices about ¼ inch thick.

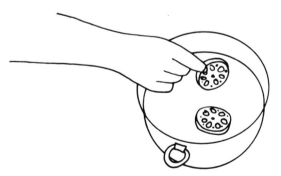

2. Soak the slices in a solution of Fruit-Fresh (mix 2 tablespoons per cup of water) to prevent them from browning.

3. Select a small hole for the eye of the peacock. Shape the head. The outline of the bird can first be etched in with a skewer.

4. Shape the rest of the bird.